Inquiries af.

INQUIRIES
after
HOMICIDE

edited by Jill Peay

Duckworth

First published in 1996 by
Gerald Duckworth & Co. Ltd.
The Old Piano Factory
48 Hoxton Square, London N1 6PB
Tel: 0171 729 5986
Fax: 0171 729 0015

Editorial arrangement © 1996 by
Suffolk Health Authority
The contributors retain copyright
in their individual chapters.

A catalogue record for this book is available
from the British Library

ISBN 0 7156 2724 4

Acknowledgments

The editor gratefully acknowledges the unfailing assistance of
Brian Morden and his team from Suffolk Health, of Jenny
Deiches at Brunel University and of Al Partington, for technical
and other support.

Typeset by Ray Davies
Printed in Great Britain by
Redwood Books Ltd, Trowbridge

Contents

Abbreviations

ACPC	Area Child Protection Committee
BASW	British Association of Social Workers
DOH	Department of Health
GMC	General Medical Council
HAS	Health Advisory Service
HMSO	Her Majesty's Stationery Office
LSE	London School of Economics and Political Science
MHRT	Mental Health Review Tribunal
MIND	National Association for Mental Health
MPS	Medical Protection Society
NHS	National Health Service
NSF	National Schizophrenia Fellowship
NSPCC	National Society for the Prevention of Cruelty to Children
PCA	Parliamentary Commissioner for Administration
RCP	Royal College of Psychiatrists
SANE	Schizophrenia A National Emergency
UKCC	United Kingdom Central Council for Nursing Midwifery and Health

Contributors

Sir Louis Blom-Cooper QC has chaired no fewer than nine public inquiries in the last ten years, most of them in the areas of child welfare and mental health. In 1991-2 he chaired the inquiry into complaints about Ashworth Hospital which led to major reforms in the running of Special Hospitals. He was Chairman of the Mental Health Act Commission from 1987 to 1994. He is a Queen's Counsel, practising in the field of Public Law. He was knighted in 1992.

David Carson Senior Lecturer in the Faculty of Law at Southampton University. His principal interests lie in the behavioural sciences and law and the prevention of legal disputes, such as by the development of risk-taking policies and procedures. In 1994 he was founding Director of the Behavioural Sciences and Law Network, which provides courses on extant inter-disciplinary topics and organises conferences on developing issues. With Professor Ray Bull, of the University of Portsmouth's Psychology Department, he is founding co-editor of the international and interdisciplinary refereed journal *Expert Evidence* and co-editor of *Handbook of Psychology in Legal Contexts* (Wiley 1995).

Sir Cecil Clothier KCB, QC Former Recorder of Blackpool and Judge of Appeal. Sir Cecil's legal career has embraced many roles, including legal assessor to the General Medical Council 1972-8 and membership of the Royal Commission on the NHS 1976-8. He was subsequently the Parliamentary Commissioner for Administration and Health Service Commissioner for England, Wales and Scotland, later Chairman of the Police Complaints Authority 1985-8, and later still Chairman of the Council on Tribunals 1989-92. Most recently, he chaired the Allitt Inquiry, relating to the deaths and injuries on the children's ward at Grantham and Kesteven General Hospital; its report was published in 1994.

John Crichton is currently a research registrar in forensic
psychiatry at Cambridge University's Institute of Criminology.
He was a student at Nottingham University where he gradu-
ated in Behavioural Science (1988) and medicine (1990). After
completing his junior psychiatric training at Fulbourn Hospital,
Cambridge, Dr Crichton was appointed the foundation Nightin-
gale Research Scholar at Trinity Hall, Cambridge. In 1994 he
was seconded onto the Robinson Inquiry as a research assistant
and later edited the proceedings of the Inquiry's academic seminar day *Psychiatric Patient Violence: Risk and Response* (Duckworth 1995). He is currently completing his PhD thesis which
investigates the nature of psychiatric control and discipline.

Sylvia Duncan is a Chartered Clinical Psychologist and
Accredited Family Therapist and works as an independent child
care consultant at the Ashwood Centre, Woking, Surrey. Her
clinical practice has developed around her work with children
and families, focussing especially on recovery from childhood
trauma. She has researched and published extensively in the
field of child protection and regularly gives expert opinions in
the courts. She is co-author of *Beyond Blame: Child Abuse
Tragedies Revisited*, which provides a systematic analysis of 35
public inquiries into cases of fatal child abuse.

Nigel Eastman is Head of the Section of Forensic Psychiatry, St George's Hospital Medical School. He is doubly qualified
as a psychiatrist and Barrister at Law and has pursued a close
interest in the relationship between psychiatry and law, pub-
lishing and giving conference papers widely on topics within the
field. He is Secretary of the Mental Health Law Sub-Committee
of the Royal College of Psychiatrists and a Member of the
Mental Health and Disability Committee of the Law Society. He
is also Assistant Editor for Legal Psychiatry of the *Psychiatric
Bulletin*, as well as being an Assistant Editor of *Advances in
Psychiatric Treatment* and of the *British Journal of Psychiatry*.
Dr Eastman is a practising Consultant Forensic Psychiatrist
and is also Advisor on services for mentally disordered offenders
to the South Thames Regional Office of the NHS Executive.

Jill Peay Senior Lecturer, Department of Law, Brunel University and Associate Tenant, Doughty Street Chambers. Dr
Peay has researched and published primarily in the field of

criminal justice. She has a particular interest in offenders suffering from mental disorder and is the author of *Tribunals on Trial: A Study of Decision-Making under the Mental Health Act 1983*. She was formerly a Research Fellow at the Oxford Centre for Criminological Research, and a Visiting Assistant Professor at Simon Fraser University, British Columbia. She sat for six years on the advisory board of the International Academy of Law and Mental Health.

Peter Reder Consultant Child and Adolescent Psychiatrist, Child and Family Consultation Centre; and Director, Centre for Relationship Studies, Riverside Mental Health Trust, London; Honorary Senior Lecturer, Charing Cross and Westminster Medical School. Dr Reder has a special research and practice interest in child protection and has published widely on this and related topics, including co-authorship of *Beyond Blame: Child Abuse Tragedies Revisited* and co-editorship of *Assessment of Parenting: Psychiatric and Psychological Contributions*. He is also an Accredited Family Therapist and on the teaching staff of the Institute of Family Therapy (London) and is associated with a number of specialist professional journals.

Paul Rock Professor of Sociology at the London School of Economics. He has written generally on criminological theory, the policy-making process in the criminal justice systems of Canada and of England and Wales and on policies and programmes for the victims of crime, and, more specifically, on the social organization of a Crown Court centre and the rebuilding of Holloway Prison. His most recent books are *Helping Victims of Crime: The Home Office and the Rise of Victim Support in England and Wales*, 1990, and *The Social World of an English Crown Court*, 1993. *Reconstructing a Women's Prison: The Holloway Redevelopment Project 1968-88* will be published in April 1996. He has taught and lectured in Canada and the United States; was Visiting Scholar at the Programs Branch of the Ministry of the Solicitor General of Canada in 1981; was a member of the Parole Board between 1986 and 1989; and has acted as a consultant to the Home Office on a number of occasions. He served as editor of the *British Journal of Sociology* between 1988 and 1995 and as Director of the Mannheim Centre

x   *Contributors*

for the Study of Criminology and Criminal Justice between 1992 and 1995.

David Sheppard is Director of the Institute of Mental Health Law and a freelance consultant who trains extensively on mental health law and practice throughout England and Wales. He was employed for seventeen years as a social worker by both inner-city and rural local authorities. As a generic and specialist mental health social worker and manager, he has worked in a variety of settings, including intake and patch teams, out-of-hours service, and psychiatric hospitals. His extensive practical experience includes twelve years as a Mental Welfare Officer and Approved Social Worker. From 1989 he worked for three years in the legal and parliamentary unit of MIND. He compiled *Learning the Lessons* a guide to mental health inquiries and their recommendations, published by the Zito Trust in January 1995; he is currently researching a follow-up publication (due Spring 1996).

Oliver Thorold is a practising barrister at Doughty Street Chambers. Specialising in mental health law (with a particular emphasis on public law ramifications) and personal injury claims in cases of medical negligence, his practice involves extensive representation before inquests, professional conduct committees, and Mental Health Review Tribunals. He has taken cases before both the European Commission and the European Court of Human Rights raising mental health and treatment issues. From 1978-81 he acted as an in-house lawyer for MIND and he now lectures regularly to mental health professionals. He acted as counsel to both the Jason Mitchell Inquiry and to one of its predecessors, the Robinson Inquiry into the death of Georgina Robinson at the Edith Morgan Centre.

John Trotter is a practising solicitor with the firm Bates, Wells & Braithwaite. For many years he has specialised in representing social work professionals at inquiries. During the 1970s and 1980s he was retained as the solicitor to the British Association of Social Workers and acted for them in all the major child abuse inquiries of that era. He continues to represent BASW and undertakes other work in administrative law, increasingly involving judicial review.

1

Introduction

Jill Peay

This edited collection, arising out of a one-day seminar held following the Independent Inquiry into the case of Jason Mitchell, brings together the views of academics, professionals and practitioners. It reviews the legal procedures and pitfalls, questions what has been learnt from 'Inquiries after Homicide' and explores what tangible benefits they bring. Moreover, it seeks to establish whether and how the hidden benefits – to those needing to understand what happened – might be weighed against the hidden costs, in particular, to those whose professional decisions are judged retrospectively.

Although the participants at the seminar day were invited to listen to presentations, the chapters in this book have been shamelessly re-worked to draw on contributions from the audience. For it was a very lively day and the 'audience' of some forty-four, together with the Independent Panel, made up a body of expertise representing the relevant professions, pressure and victims' groups, academics, health service administrators, civil servants, mental health experts and the media. Many came wearing more than one hat; members of previous or ongoing Inquiries also attended. It was a sophisticated audience, invited because they would be vocal and reflective. We have tried to embrace, if not reconcile, their varied perspectives. As is the way with such events, the seminar day raised more questions without fully answering those it had posed. The very nature of the topic and the diverse audience invited perhaps made this inevitable.

At one level, the role of the 'Inquiry after Homicide' appears straightforward. Public concern about an incident generates the

need for an Inquiry to elicit, in the words of Sir Louis Blom-
Cooper QC

> the truth ... what happened; how did it happen; and who, if
> anybody, was responsible, culpably or otherwise, for it having
> happened.[1]

Their terms of reference fix the nature and extent of their
investigations and should rein in any untoward desire to popu-
larise their subject matter or stray into general areas of policy
or politics.

However, 'Inquiries after Homicide' take on a life of their
own. They are not an event, but a social process. They examine
not a single decision and its wisdom or lack of it, but the
interaction of a series of decisions and omissions and their
consequences, and yet further courses of action, adopted or
neglected, taken by a range of people whose responsibilities
overlap, occur sequentially or merely run parallel to, possibly in
ignorance of, one another. Indeed, the very existence of 'Inquiries after Homicide' cannot be separated from the impact they
have upon those of whom they inquire, those who document and
report the proceedings and those who merely listen. In this
guise, Inquiries can take on, or be attributed with, many functions that diverge from their formal role. Even within their own
terms of reference, some matters evolve, taking precedence over
others during the time span of the Inquiry. This can produce a
mushrooming of observations and recommendations few could
have anticipated in the preparatory stages. For it is only during
the process of the Inquiry, once the panel members have had a
chance to digest the wealth of documentation, that the real
questions will emerge.

Another area of uncertainty then arises. How far should
Inquiries go in attempting to answer both their formal terms of
reference and the additional emergent questions? Indeed, how
do they know not only when they have secured enough documentation, questioned enough witnesses and unearthed enough
information, but also whether there is 'sufficient' to answer
questions with any particular degree of certainty? In short, how
confident do they need to be of the reliability and validity of their

observations? Moreover, should Inquiries embrace 'why' as well as 'what' type questions if culpability is an issue? This overall lack of clarity and purpose can result in Inquiries becoming all things to all people; this chameleon-like quality can result in an explosion of the time, effort and resources devoted to them with an arguable dilution of their original objectives. In turn, this makes much more difficult any attempt to quantify the true financial cost of the Inquiry and any lost opportunity costs.

If the seminar came to any conclusions I would suggest a broad concordance with the view that in their current form, 'Inquiries after Homicide' are a dying breed; in short, they must adapt, evolve or change. Disaggregation of function was much discussed – separating aspects of individual responsibility and discipline from the generic issues the Inquiry faced – those of learning lessons, recommending reforms, training matters and the crucial role Inquiries can play as a form of catharsis for secondary victims. There was also a recognition of, if not agreement with, the need for greater procedural regularity and predictability, possibly with a standing secretariat, but certainly with some rules of engagement. The Chairman of the Commission for Local Administration spoke persuasively of the pre-investigation procedures and statutory remit of the Ombudsman; those involved with and having acute memories of the child abuse inquiries of the 1970s and '80s spoke of the way in which those inquiries had taken on a new form. Other models were alluded to; the role of the Coroner's Inquest was seen as too circumscribed, but Scottish Fatal Accident Inquiries might bear further examination. The unpreparedness of witnesses, the apprehension as to what they might face, the uncertainty the Inquiry confronted as to whether it would gain access to medical records and if so, whether that access, based as it must be on the patient's consent, might thereafter be withdrawn; all of these were the down-side of an informal, non-statutory footing for an Inquiry.

The need for change has also been recognised by the Department of Health.[2] The Department had independently been considering the need to fine tune some of its recommended procedures for 'Inquiries after Homicide', and had already begun to take a longer look at how such Inquiries should evolve.

The seminar day, at which the Department was represented, provided further momentum to this process of reappraisal. The Department had not been wedded to the current form of Inquiries, and, provided any modifications preserved the primary objective of the Executive Guidance – summarised by them as 'to protect the public and patients' – the view was taken that there was sufficient flexibility within the Guidance to permit change.[3] Thus, although Inquiries were mandatory, their form was not, given that they remained independent of the service providers.

In this context the Department now favoured devolving responsibility for the detailed operation of individual Inquiries away from the centre, to its Regional Offices, provided that it was clearly spelt out which parties should benefit from an Inquiry and what their purpose was (in itself, no mean feat if it could be achieved). Moreover, the Department took very seriously the desirability of not bundling together a series of issues that were better left disaggregated. Thus, issues of discipline, catharsis, learning lessons and training matters were probably best dealt with in different but specialised fora, or at different times.

It would perhaps be insensitive to suggest that not all homicides need a full Independent Inquiry, for it seems to imply that one death may be more worthy of examination than another – all will leave bewildered secondary victims in their wake – victims in need of some kind of explanation. But equally, the examination of near deaths or suicides may produce telling lessons of greater general applicability.[4] It is not clear whether we wish to learn from Inquiries or to learn about the events they explore; nor is it clear that relatives and friends would necessarily favour the latter goal over the former – for as Paul Rock's chapter details, many secondary victims share a common desire that what has happened to them should not happen to others – hence the need for general and preventive lessons to be learnt.

Another notable feature of the seminar day was the way in which apparently conflicting positions – for example, the debate about whether such proceedings are best held in public or private – emerged on closer inspection to share some common ground, while for other elements the disputed areas were better delineated. For example, the seductive nature of proceedings in private was argued by some to be the best basis for getting at the truth. In one memorable exchange the case was put that witnesses are, like patients, more prepared to undress in the privacy of a doctor's surgery; the riposte was telling – would they be as prepared if they knew that a photograph was to be taken and reproduced in public? Whichever way the conflict might be resolved by argument, it was evident that the wishes of those paying for the Inquiry could not be ignored – in a sense, they held the trump card. Joanna Spicer, the Chairman of Suffolk Health, shared her concerns with the participants at the seminar day. She argued persuasively that those in public life, like herself, who were responsible for public funds had to be accountable. Thus, she argued, if an Inquiry were to be held in private there must be clear and demonstrable reasons for so doing. In essence, there had to be ownership of a decision by the commissioning authority following an informed debate. She had no regrets about holding the Jason Mitchell Inquiry in public, despite having to run the gauntlet of media attention.

The format of this book broadly follows that of the seminar held on 3 November 1995. The first chapter sets 'Inquiries after Homicide' in their historical context and in the broader framework of tribunals and inquiries as a legal species. It also introduces the questions posed at the seminar day; these had been sent to all participants in order to ensure that some pre-emptive thinking had been undertaken – both by the other speakers and by the audience. Oliver Thorold and John Trotter were set the task of producing a check-list of issues to be considered by any body faced with the daunting task of establishing an 'Inquiry after Homicide'. Theirs was designed as a 'nuts and bolts piece' in the spirit of 'everything you wished you had known before ...'. However, their chapter goes beyond this remit and reflects upon the advantages of a statutory basis for Inquiries, particularly vis-à-vis the vexed issue of medical confidentiality – one which the Independent Inquiry into the case of Jason Mitchell has explored extensively. The contribution by Sir Cecil Clothier propounds the merits of private as opposed to public hearings. The other side of the coin had been put on the seminar day by Ann Alexander; these two had previously encountered one another at the Beverley Allitt Inquiry where Ann Alexander had represented some of the victims' families. Sir Louis Blom-Cooper, who chaired the Independent Panel of Inquiry into the Jason Mitchell case and responded on behalf of the Panel at the seminar day, offers some reflections of his own on Public Inquiries. He asks rhetorically whether the 'expansive and expensive method' of an inquiry can be justified in terms of the aims and purpose of good government? The affirmative answer which follows is, however, substantially qualified. John Crichton and Dave Sheppard's 'Learning the Lessons' constitutes an indictment of the impotence of the various Inquiries' recommendations. It can come as no surprise that one Inquiry after another treads the same ground when their reports are physically inaccessible in a variety of ways those at the seminar day found disturbing. The authors conclude with ten practical suggestions for reform of 'Inquiries after Homicide'. The chapter by Peter Reder and Sylvia Duncan makes one of the most important contributions to the way forward, since it draws on their experience of child abuse inquiries to make recommendations for separating out the various functions of 'Inquiries after Homicide'. This, they argue, would assist Inquiries to go 'Beyond Blame' into the more constructive process of determining how homicides as an event can be understood. In essence, one aspect of their argument is that there are too many distracting and incompatible agendas at an Inquiry for this function of 'understanding' to be tackled properly. Paul Rock's chapter, based on his empirical work with secondary victims of homicide, powerfully reminds those in the field of the overwhelming and all-embracing impact that this form of bereavement can have, and of the shabby way in which these victims can be treated. Their clear sense of grievance is not for themselves, nor is it vituperative, but it can lead to organizing and campaigning to prevent any others from suffering in the same way. The last two chapters question whether Inquiries may be doing more harm than good in their present form. David Carson's trenchant critique addresses the doubtful decision-making strategies of the Inquiries and elaborates on many of the problems alluded to above concerning the nature of the questions Inquiries pose for themselves. Do Inquiries merely tread a well-worn path asking the most obvious questions without fully addressing more inaccessible issues of resources and management strategies? Nigel Eastman's chapter reflects much of the professional disquiet about Inquiries, and, drawing on his rare dual perspective, he is able forcibly to propound the view that issues of culpability should properly be left to the appropriate fora, namely the courts and the respective professional bodies. He calls for the abolition of mandatory 'Inquiries after Homicide', an uncoupling of the explanatory and disciplinary purposes and much else besides. Crucially, though, he argues that there should now be established an ongoing audit of these Inquiries, to determine their future in the context of a full analytical exposition of their role.

The interaction between the seminar day, the Report of the Jason Mitchell Panel of Inquiry and the ultimate future of 'Inquiries after Homicide' has yet fully to play itself out. It is important, however, to pay tribute to the contribution of Paul Bowden. Although his paper is not reproduced here, it captured in telling form the reasons for and depth of anger he experienced, as a psychiatrist, about some 'Inquiries after Homicide'. The influence his critique had, and continues to have, is impossible to quantify; but it would be untrue to assert that the Jason Mitchell Panel were untouched by Dr Bowden's critique.

Finally, it is important to acknowledge not only the role played by Suffolk Health in agreeing to sponsor the seminar day and this publication, but also that of the Independent Panel of Inquiry, in subjecting itself to a critical and reflective process. Not all the papers concluded that Inquiries were a good thing, or even that they did a good job. To accept that one doesn't know and certainly doesn't know best may be a sufficient first step.

Notes

1. Blom-Cooper L. (1993) 'Public inquiries', in M. Freeman and B. Hepple (eds) *Current Legal Problems Vol. 46 Part II Collected Papers*, Oxford University Press, at 206.

2. Personal communication with a representative of the Mental Health and Community Care Division, Department of Health on 23 November 1995.

3. Department of Health (1994) *Guidance on the discharge of men-*

tally disordered people and their continuing care in the community
NHS Executive HSG(94)27 ~~and LASSL(94)4~~ 10 May 1994. See also
Appendix A where selected sections of the Guidance are reproduced in
full.

4. A joint report prepared by the Mental Health Act Commission and
the Division of Psychiatry and Psychology at the United Medical and
Dental Schools, South London, has noted that of 200 deaths of compul-
sorily detained patients over a two-year period, 95 were probable
suicides, some of which could have been prevented; see (1995) *Deaths
of Detained Patients*, Mental Health Foundation (37 Mortimer Street,
London).

Themes and Questions:
The Inquiry in Context

Jill Peay

Homicides by those who have received care from mental health
services are rare events. Multiple homicides rarer still. Their
impact, however, is far-reaching. The tragedy of violent death is
followed by dislocation and despair for families – both of victim
and perpetrator – while the professionals involved and the
community as a whole can be variously touched by anger, anguish and self-reproach.

Since the publication of the NHS Executive Guidance in 1994,
Inquiries into such events are now inevitable.[1] The section of the
Guidance headed 'If things go wrong' outlines the necessary
procedures where a violent incident occurs. Paragraph 34
states:

> ... after the completion of any legal proceedings it may be neces-
> sary to hold an independent inquiry. **In cases of homicide, it
> will always be necessary to hold an inquiry which is inde-
> pendent of the providers involved**.[2]

But what is the proper role of 'Inquiries after Homicide' and
what are their achievements and shortcomings? This chapter
provides a context for those that follow by placing 'Inquiries
after Homicide' in the framework of the role of Inquiries as a
whole. It briefly reviews the background to the Jason Mitchell
Inquiry, explores the potential and varied impact of Inquiries
and concludes with the series of questions posed on the seminar
day about the function of such Inquiries.

Central to this discussion is a recognition that the Inquiry process shifts the focus of interest from the perpetrator to the decisions and actions of those previously responsible for his care, treatment and management; significantly more often than not, it is a 'he'.[3] It may seem paradoxical, particularly to the secondary victims – relatives and friends of the deceased – that exploration of the perpetrator's motives and his responsibility for what has occurred appears peripheral to the Inquiry's remit. This can be galling where the perpetrator's 'day in court' will probably already have been curtailed: first by a guilty plea;[4] and secondly by the relative rapidity with which the plea follows the incident. Thus, whatever mental disorder the perpetrator may have been suffering from, it as likely as not continues in any court proceedings to impair the full exploration and understanding of his part in the tragedy. It is the system of care, and crucially, the actors within it who take centre stage at an Inquiry.

Shifting the focus of attention in this way has a profound impact on the professionals involved. Even the most efficient of Inquiry Panels can take months to establish, collating all the necessary documentation and marshalling witnesses; weeks to hear the evidence; and then further months to consider their views, draw appropriate conclusions and publish a report. During this period the potential for paralysis, recriminations and defensive practices is considerable and a pervasively anxious atmosphere can set in amongst those subject to the Inquiry process. Given that most patients and former patients will have had contact with multiple agencies over the years, the Inquiry's desire to root out the sequence of events preceding the tragedy will touch the lives of many individuals continuing professionally to care for others with mental health needs.

Although only a small number of Inquiries have so far reported some 30 are potentially in the pipeline.[5] Such figures should come as no surprise, for an annual homicide rate in this country of some 600-700 will inevitably entail killings by people suffering from mental disorder. The Boyd Report *identified* 34 homicides, committed over a three-year period, where there had been contact by the perpetrator with the psychiatric services in the preceding twelve months.[6] One forensic psychiatrist has argued that, given the prevalence of mental health problems, some 50 homicides every year might be expected by current sufferers.[7] Of course, of those 50 only a proportion will have formally been known to have had psychiatric problems.[8] And of those, only a proportion will fall within the Health Service Guidance as being 'discharged patients' where an Inquiry is mandatory.[9] But, with an Inquiry to follow each homicide, it would not take long before all purchasing health authorities – of which there are some 96 – either had been subject to an Inquiry, were undergoing one, awaiting one or merely holding their collective breath for the inevitable death to trigger the Inquiry process.

Questioning of professional judgment – questioning which takes place with the benefit of hindsight and in the context of the exceptional circumstances of homicide or multiple homicide – lies at the heart of the inquiry process. Could the perpetrator's behaviour and the ultimate tragedy have been predicted or prevented? Should more care have been taken? Could mistakes have been avoided? But the forensic search for answers, seductive as it may be, is deceptively misleading. Subject to this level of analysis, which of us would be likely to be found completely without fault? Even where errors of judgment can be retrospectively demonstrated to have been compounded by further errors, what real significance do they have? For these are the correlates of the homicide, not necessarily its cause. Is shifting the focus in this way for one form of offending – and it is significant that such Inquiries do not inevitably follow other incidents of homicide – antithetical to a 'true' understanding of events? Do such 'Inquiries after Homicide' explain, expose, expiate or merely excoriate?

Tribunals, inquiries and tribunals of inquiry

It is not unusual for me to tell my public law students, having covered in detail judicial review and the ombudsman, something to the effect that 'there are, of course, a series of other non-judicial methods of controlling administrative action, including tribunals, inquiries etc. Indeed, there are 71 different types of tribunal alone listed in Wade on Administrative Law.[10] You need not bother with attempting to get to grips with their range and form. It suffices for you to know they exist and to remember that tribunals make significantly more decisions than the civil courts.'

This statement is misleading. It is my intention to grapple with tribunals and inquiries and locate the 'Inquiry after Homicide' in its proper context. This is not an easy task, for both the language and lines of demarcation between these various bodies are confusing. Moreover, the *Tribunals and Inquiries Act 1992* (and its forerunners the 1958 and 1971 Acts) makes many of the procedural safeguards employed of common origin; even Wraith and Lamb's seminal study of Public Inquiries deals with special types of inquiry which can be, and often are, held in private.[11]

(a) Statutory tribunals and inquiries

Wade and Forsyth draw a functional distinction between statutory tribunals and inquiries; the former, they argue, make judicial decisions by applying legal rules to self-contained issues, while inquiries, although similarly engaged in a fact-finding exercise, will make recommendations – usually to a minister – on a matter not amenable to pure legal resolution.[12] Thus, inquiries are preliminary to administrative or political decisions; they serve, in a quasi-judicial manner, to ensure that administrative power is fairly and reasonably exercised and that citizens' feelings are assuaged. This is achieved by ensuring that the local aspects of a potentially larger issue involving matters of public policy can be taken into account by the ultimate decision-maker. Whether such local aspects are ultimately persuasive is, of course, another matter. Tribunals may also be distinguished from inquiries in that the former enjoy a more permanent existence and a defined area of jurisdiction; inquiries are constituted ad hoc – the very term, as Wraith and Lamb note,

> is used loosely for convenience, and may denote anything from a piece of administrative routine to a major public inquisition.[13]

(b) Statutory inquiries

Although the content of statutory inquiries may relate to administrative functions as varied as parking adjudication and the national lottery, their form may be broadly divided into three types:

- the true statutory inquiry – like planning inquiries – held under a statutory duty
- discretionary statutory inquiries – for example, under the *Education Act 1979*
- accident inquiries – held under statute, but not the *Tribunals and Inquiries Act 1992*. For example, s.466 of the *Merchant Shipping Act 1894* gives powers to hold an inquiry where ships collide at sea.

(c) Tribunals of Inquiry

These 'extra-legal' inquiries require parliamentary authorization under the *Tribunals of Inquiry (Evidence) Act 1921*. Clothed with the powers of the High Court and presided over by an eminent judge, some nineteen have been held since the Act was passed, perhaps most famously dealing with the Aberfan disaster, the leaking of budget secrets, and espionage matters arising out of the Vassall case. Tribunals of Inquiry, described by Segal as 'a British contribution to the legal world',[14] are intended to examine alleged misdeeds by ministers of the Crown, civil servants, local authorities and the police. They have been held primarily in the context of some 'emergency', where a nationwide crisis of confidence needed to be allayed. Wraith and Lamb regard them as

> well-publicized inquisitions on the grand scale, not concerned with government policy and administration but, for the most part, with the investigation of suspected impropriety or negligence in public life.[15]

Although Tribunals of Inquiry are concerned to discover

what has happened, and, if necessary, to recommend how to

prevent its recurrence ... the restoration of public confidence is
an objective of paramount importance.[16]

Curiously, the Profumo affair, seemingly ripe for a Tribunal of
Inquiry, was subject rather to a private investigation by Lord
Denning in which he acted as 'detective, solicitor, counsel and
judge'.[17] In the aftermath of the Profumo affair a Royal Commission (chaired by Lord Justice Salmon) was set up to review the
Tribunals of Inquiry (Evidence) Act 1921. It reported in 1966,
making some 50 recommendations, in particular relating to the
safeguards afforded to the participants at an Inquiry. Six cardinal principles emerged.

1. Before any person becomes involved in an inquiry, the
tribunal must be satisfied that there are circumstances which
affect him and which the tribunal proposes to investigate.

2. Before any person who is involved in an inquiry is called as
a witness, he should be informed of any allegations which are
made against him and the substance of the evidence in support
of them.

3(a) He should be given an adequate opportunity of preparing
his case and of being assisted by legal advisers.

3(b) His legal expenses should normally be met out of public
funds.

4. He should have the opportunity of being examined by his
own solicitor or counsel and stating his case in public at the
inquiry.

5. Any material witnesses he wishes called at the inquiry
should, if reasonably practicable, be heard.

6. He should have the opportunity of testing by cross-examination, conducted by his own solicitor or counsel, any evidence
which may affect him.[18]

These principles have never formally been brought into effect;
however, their flavour has permeated many a subsequent inquiry and the issuing of 'Salmon letters' is now commonplace.[19]
These letters, usually sent in advance of an Inquiry to witnesses
who may be subject to criticism, set out the particulars of any
allegations, thereby giving notice to the witness in an attempt

to facilitate fairness – notoriously difficult to attain in inquisitorial proceedings. For the Tribunal of Inquiry, as Wraith and Lamb note, enjoys powers

> to enforce the attendance of witnesses, and production of documents, to examine witnesses on oath and to certify recalcitrants to the High Court for contempt.[20]

Such powers of inquisition, employed in a context where Tribunals of Inquiry normally sit in public, can result in witnesses finding themselves potentially the subject of

> allegations made ... in the full glare of publicity, without proper opportunity to prepare answers to what has been said about them.[21]

Moreover, as their remit is often wide-ranging, problems unanticipated in the original terms of reference can arise. Hence the need for and derivation of Salmon's six cardinal principles.

The most recent *exception* to a 'Tribunal of Inquiry' under the 1921 Act is the Scott Inquiry into the 'Arms to Iraq' affair. Sir Richard Scott described his Inquiry as 'ad hoc'. In an address to the Chancery Bar, before the publication of his report, he was explicitly critical of the importation by the six cardinal principles of adversarial procedures into what are primarily inquisitorial inquiries.[22] To achieve fairness in such inquiries, he did not believe it necessary – indeed, he regarded it as a positive impediment – to have full procedural safeguards, wherein every witness was represented and had the opportunity to cross-examine all other witnesses. He argued that much of the procedural morass could be overcome by allowing witnesses to comment and correct in writing, from the privacy of their own offices, as advised if necessary by their own lawyers.[23] This procedure has, of course, led to the usual mountain of documentation becoming a positive range.

(d) Non-statutory inquiries

In a non-statutory inquiry the objector/citizen enjoys no procedural rights beyond the general reach of natural justice. Although Crichel Down, Stansted and Sizewell B are among the best known of the major non-statutory inquiries, such inquiries are frequently employed by specific bodies; for example, the serious fraud office of the Department of Trade Inspectors.[24] But, with no obligation to hold them in public, to publish evidence or even any emergent report, non-statutory inquiries are potentially fatally flawed as a means of allaying public disquiet.

Criticisms of the inquiries held by the Department of Trade Inspectors featured prominently in the House of Lords debate on 'Inquisitional Inquiries'; for example, Lord Boardman expressed concern that this form of inquiry frequently examined allegations of misconduct, yet those subject to inquiry did not necessarily enjoy all or any of the procedural protections associated with adversarial judicial proceedings in court settings.[25] Moreover, because an inquiry's proceedings are not *sub judice* selective media reporting could enhance the perceived and actual injustices they embody. Lord Lester detailed eight features which made the inquiries 'unsatisfactory and unfair':[26]

- no presumption of innocence
- secret proceedings
- no prescribed procedures
- witnesses need not be identified to those subject to investigation
- no entitlement to cross-examination or access to documentary evidence
- inspectors may rely upon 'inadmissible' evidence
- the Secretary of State may publish the report under the Companies Act even though reputations may be destroyed
- no right of appeal or effective access to any court to challenge the findings

Although, in practice, most of these criticisms do not apply to 'Inquiries after Homicide', all potentially can apply to its non-statutory form. It is these due process shortcomings which many would argue form the basis of the critique of 'Inquiries after Homicide'. Whether greater procedural safeguards would inhibit the Inquiry's 'quest for the truth', or whether they could enhance witnesses' preparedness to co-operate, is central to the discussion in this book and, in particular, to the debate as to whether inquiries should be held in public or private and on a statutory or non-statutory basis. Here also is the tension within non-statutory inquiries between the desire for openness, embodied in publication and access to the report, and the desire not to condemn publicly on the basis of flawed procedures. This critique thus begins to raise an argument in favour of reforming such inquisitional inquiries by disaggregating their various functions. Requiring an inquiry to make general and specific recommendations, to seek the truth and create a basis for identifying individual failure may simply be asking it to undertake too many conflicting and irreconcilable functions. Hence the proposals in favour of disaggregation explored at length in other chapters.

(e) Inquiries after Homicide

These are arguably a sub-species of non-statutory inquiry. Perhaps the true fore-runners of the 'Inquiry after Homicide' are first, a series of statutory inquiries starting in the late 1960s into the mistreatment of mainly geriatric or mentally handicapped patients, and secondly, the child abuse inquiries of the 1970s and '80s.[27] The 22 hospital inquiry reports, published between 1969 and 1981, and the central issue they raised of how institutions established to care could have permitted neglect, callousness and deliberate cruelty, were critically reviewed by John Martin in his book 'Hospitals in Trouble'.[28] The child abuse inquiries were the subject of Reder *et al.*'s *Beyond Blame* and create a context for Peter Reder and Sylvia Duncan's chapter in this edited collection.[29] Both these earlier books explore in detail the problems which have arisen, phoenix-like, in a new guise in 'Inquiries after Homicide'.

It is possible for 'Inquiries after Homicide' to be invested with statutory powers by the Secretary of State for Health under s.125 of the *Mental Health Act 1983*. This can occur in any case where the Secretary of State thinks it

> advisable to do so in connection with any matter arising under this Act.

However, the Jason Mitchell Inquiry was a non-statutory inquiry, as have been all the other Inquiries held under the NHS Executive Guidance.

'Inquiries after Homicide' also bear a superficial resemblance to Tribunals of Inquiry, in that they have most recently arisen in the context of 'much public disquiet'. Yet this context of 'public disquiet' has arguably been built upon, if not generated by, the priorities of the popular press. Fundamentally, 'Inquiries after Homicide' arise in the context of private tragedy, in a set of unique circumstances about which there may be few general lessons to be learnt. Although parallels with inquiries into the abuse and neglect of children are pertinent, can the position of children and those using the mental health services truly be equated? It could be argued that the public have a proper locus in child abuse cases, where the presumption is that children (and babies) cannot be expected to fend for themselves, whereas the treatment (or refusal to accept treatment) of adult psychiatric patients starts from the premise that their wishes are to be respected. Although these wishes may not necessarily be regarded by the relevant professionals as being in the patient's best interests, unless a patient's judgment is so impaired as to bring him or her within the ambit of compulsory treatment, these wishes – at least in the negative sense – should be determinative. Thus the setting is fundamentally private and treatment subject to the usual restraints of medical confidentiality.

Locating the context of 'Inquiries after Homicide' is, however, the easy task. Deciding upon their role, given the range of models they might adopt, is much more difficult.

Background to the Jason Mitchell Inquiry

Jason Mitchell tendered guilty pleas on the basis of diminished responsibility to the manslaughter of Arthur Wilson, Shirley Wilson and Robert Mitchell.[30] These offences were committed shortly before Christmas 1994 when Jason Mitchell went missing from Easton House, part of St Clement's Hospital, Ipswich. His status there was that of an informal patient in the rehabilitation area. Born in 1970, Jason Mitchell had a history of both in-patient psychiatric treatment and of periods in custody following criminal convictions. On 7 July 1995 he received three concurrent sentences of life imprisonment. He is currently detained in Rampton Special Hospital.

The broad terms of the Jason Mitchell Inquiry were '**to examine and assess the quality of the care and control that Jason Mitchell received in the years and months leading up to his absence on December 9th 1994**'.

Para 36 of the NHS Executive 'Guidance on the discharge of mentally disordered people and their continuing care in the community' deals with three issues to be taken into account in setting up an independent inquiry following homicide.

   i. **the remit of the inquiry** should encompass at least:
      – the care the patient was receiving at the time of the incident;
      – the suitability of that care in view of the patient's history and assessed health and social needs;
      – the extent to which that care corresponded with statutory obligations, relevant guidance from the Department of Health, and local operational policies;
      – the exercise of professional judgement;
      – the adequacy of the care plan and its monitoring by the key worker

  ii. **composition of the inquiry panel.** Consideration should be given to appointing a lawyer as chairman. Other members should include a psychiatrist and a senior social services manager and/or a senior nurse. No member of the panel should be employed by bodies responsible for the care of the patient

iii. **distribution of the inquiry report.** Although it will not always be desirable for the final report to be made public, an undertaking should be given at the start of the inquiry that its main findings will be made available to interested parties'

The role of the Inquiry

It is indicative of the lack of clarity as to the role and function of 'Inquiries after Homicide' that those involved with the preparation of the seminar found it difficult to agree on a title. We explored a number of different epithets; explanation, exposition, exculpation, exoneration, expiation, excoriation, exhortation, extenuation, extrication .... And I could well now add expatiation (to write copiously, wander unrestrainedly). In the end, exposition and expiation were chosen, but the list remained deliberately open.

My own research into the operation of Mental Health Review Tribunals noted that tribunals fulfil a number of subsidiary roles beyond that strictly interpreted as being a legal safeguard for patients.[31] They could act as a catalyst, a lever, a conduit for information, a resource for the professionals involved in care and a therapeutic tool. As with MHRTs, the 'Inquiry after Homicide' will have a number of formal and informal roles, some conflicting. Moreover, not all will necessarily be anticipated. For example, Jason Mitchell was reluctant to communicate with the Inquiry Panel in its early days; he was similarly reported by his responsible medical officer at Rampton Hospital, Dr Wilson, to be markedly wary of him. Yet, as the Inquiry progressed, Jason Mitchell did speak at length with two of the Panel, Dr Grounds and Mrs Guinan, in the full knowledge that his disclosures would not remain confidential and would be passed on to the team responsible for his care at Rampton. Whether these disclosures were genuine (whatever that might mean) or an opportunity for him to present his version of events to a wider audience and/or to manipulate those around him, has been questioned, particularly by those responsible for his care immediately before the homicides. None the less, it was a role the Inquiry played, wittingly or unwittingly.

There is a central paradox underpinning the potential impact of the Inquiry and the effectiveness of its varied roles discussed below. On the one hand, Inquiries bring publicity which has the capacity to identify shortcomings and arguably to raise the quality of care of mentally disordered people in the community. On the other hand, this publicity can be counter-productive by reinforcing the resilient and pre-existing association in the minds of the public with respect to the link between mental disorder and the perpetration of violent crime upon strangers. In reality, all research evidence suggests that this link is spurious, other than in very limited circumstances.[32] This is not to deny that a link exists at all, for recent, properly resourced and methodologically sound research has indicated that the risk of violence is greater amongst the actively psychotic than the population as a whole.[33] However, it is important to stress that this increase in risk is only half that associated with alcohol and one third of the increase among those who abuse drugs.[34] However, these latter groups have not acquired the attributions of risk made to the mentally ill by media and public alike. Moreover, anything which highlights this link can undermine the public's willingness to support 'care in the community', thus further alienating the mentally disordered offender from the very community to whom the Guidance looks for safe and successful care.

(a) Raising standards – allocating resources

The NHS Guidance was introduced in the context of media and ministerial concern that community care might not be working.[35] One of its objectives was to promote a programme of care for psychiatric patients both during their stay in hospital and following discharge. Where this programme failed to prevent subsequent incidents involving death, an inquiry could, first, restore public confidence and assuage public disquiet, by demonstrating the seriousness with which the matters were perceived; and, secondly, serve to identify shortcomings, if any, in the provision of local services and thereby, where possible, facilitate an improvement in their quality.

However, this 'beefing up' of services may be more of an aspirational goal than one truly within reach for those involved with community care. For there is no necessary direct link between those to whom the report is furnished – in the case of 'Inquiries after Homicide', the purchasing authority – and the bodies identified as being deficient in some manner. For example, the Jason Mitchell Inquiry is critical of some of the internal procedures at C3, a department within the Home Office dealing with restricted patients. But what can Suffolk Health, in this instance, do to remedy such deficiencies? Exhortation, as Martin amply illustrates, remains the main option.[36] Equally, it is not uncommon for Inquiry Reports to criticise poor communication between the various caring agencies – whether statutory or voluntary; yet care in the community of necessity entails a longer leash than hospital care, making quality communication inherently problematic. Once in the community, many people will have semi-professional dealings with ex-patients without necessarily having the requisite expertise to react adequately to potentially dangerous situations.[37] In essence, control is only really feasible in conditions of some restraint and even then is not fail-safe, as the death of Georgina Robinson testifies.[38] Finally, it is notable that when the Woodley Inquiry sought to criticise the nascent 'supervised discharge orders', one element of the then *Mental Health (Patients in the Community) Bill*, as likely to cloak crucial deficiencies in services, it was condemned by John Bowis, the junior minister responsible for mental health policy, as having misunderstood the government's proposals.[39] As Martin notes

> complex social institutions have a life of their own which is not an easy target for radical reform. Most social groups tend to conservatism in wanting to preserve their own existence and, by implication, most of the circumstances which allow them to exist.[40]

Continuing care in a non-institutional setting is difficult to define, slippery to reform and amorphous in its perceived ability to absorb resources at the expense of other more easily identifiable targets. The desire to raise specific standards through the medium of a report constitutes one of an Inquiry's most tenuous objectives.

It would also be unwise, however, to ignore the impact that

first the tragedy, and then the Inquiry, can have on those most intimately affected in their desires to ensure that no others should similarly suffer. Highly motivated individuals have a remarkable ability to generate momentum for change – documented by Paul Rock's chapter in this book on the organising power of grief. For example, Jayne Zito, Jonathan Zito's widow, has been the driving force behind the establishment of the Zito Trust, which is working to improve the provision of community care for the severely mentally ill and to establish a network of support for the victims of the failure of care. Her aim, as recorded in the Clunis Report, is 'not to ensure that dangerous or potentially dangerous mentally ill people are locked up'.[41] Jayne Zito wants them to have proper care so that they and the public may be safe. Then, she feels, her husband will not have died in vain. Raising standards for all might obviate the need for at least some of the glut of current inquiries.

(b) Fact-finding – attributions of responsibility

A more traditional role for the Inquiry is that envisaged by Sir Louis Blom-Cooper. He has argued that strictly their role is 'to establish the facts so that action may be taken'.[42] Indeed, he contrasts the objective of civil litigation – an adjudication between two parties based on selective presentations of evidence, where one must win and one lose – with the role of the public inquiry, as being precisely

> to elicit the truth ... what happened; how did it happen; and who, if anybody, was responsible, culpably or otherwise, for it having happened.[43]

Moreover, he recognises that one of the strands in this combined function for Inquiries is

> to provide the symbolic purpose of holding up to obloquy that particular event that induced the crisis of public confidence.[44]

Questions of culpability can emerge with great force during the progress of an inquisitorial Inquiry and are likely further to be highlighted in the presentation and dissemination of the report.

Jill Peay

The combination of an inquisitorial approach with public hearings can place witnesses in an unenviable position. As Sir Richard Scott has noted

> There is no doubt that a public hearing...exposes witnesses to considerable pressures .... Is that fair? ... witnesses ... should not be subjected to those pressures unless the public interest factors that favour public hearings are clearly apparent and are of evident weight.[45]

It is, of course, hard to dissent from Blom-Cooper's view that

> Private citizens may expect optimum protection; those who are public servants expect to undergo public scrutiny and accountability for their actions.[46]

Indeed, Sir Richard Scott explicitly endorses this position. However, it leaves open what constitutes the definition of a public servant. In an era when many of the responsibilities of government and the civil service have been passed on to executive agencies, privatised bodies and, particularly in the caring professions, voluntary bodies, on which side of the public/private divide do these individuals stand or fall? Indeed, when the very mechanisms of inquiry and accountability, select committees and Parliament, can be outmanoeuvred through resort to the notion that 'civil servants' may be constrained in their answers because they are not independent agents, what value has public scrutiny? Finally, different professions may be answerable in different ways; is a consultant psychiatrist in a publicly funded hospital who is treating a restricted patient, where the restriction order has been made for the protection of the public but responsibility for treatment has passed to the doctor, acting within the confines of the doctor-patient relationship and the constraints of medical confidentiality, when he/she errs? Or is he/she acting as a public servant, whose medical advice will influence those charged with the public responsibility of making decisions about discharge – notably MHRTs and C3 division at the Home Office? Similarly, when a social worker breaches what would otherwise be a confidential consultation because a client has provided information which indicates there is 'clear evidence of serious danger to the client, the worker, other person or the community' are they acting in a 'public' capacity?[47] If they lack knowledge of the British Association of Social Workers' Code of Ethics or are not members of the Association – provisos which Palmer argues apply widely – are they acting in a private capacity when they fail to breach the confidential nature of the relationship, even though this may constitute a vital error in the chain of causation?[48] These are not easy questions.

(c) Blaming and shaming: a social process

There can be little doubt that the Inquiry is a powerful means of labelling behaviour as good or evil and creating a forum for shaming. Cynics might argue that although the Inquiry engenders an appearance of impartiality, integrity and accountability, 'it carries with it the danger of all show trials that it is directed to a predetermined result'.[49]

Looking at the role of one form of Inquiry in Australia, Robertson, citing Adrian Roden QC (one of the Assistant Commissioners responsible for reports by the Independent Commission Against Corruption), has noted that if the Commission is going to make legal or quasi-legal decisions about individuals (namely, findings of 'guilt' of corrupt conduct) then there should be a proper appeal process. But Robertson further cites Roden's argument that it were better that they didn't do it at all. Thus, rather than

> exposing and punishing individual acts of impropriety or corruption [that they examine] the systemic causes of such conduct and the means whereby its recurrence can be prevented. The investigation of individual conduct provides an understanding of the problem, rather than an end in itself.[50]

This analysis of the role of an inquiry in another jurisdiction is mirrored by Reder *et al.*'s analysis of child abuse inquiries in this country.[51] Thus, they argue, although we all wish to learn constructively from tragedy, an inquiry panel is set up primarily to dissipate social anxiety. It tends in consequence to reflect a compulsion in society to attribute blame. Witnesses accordingly experience the inquiry as adversarial and the final reports as judgmental. Reder *et al.* challenge the presumption that there is a truth to be found by inquiries.

> Whatever social or political pressures there were on inquiry panels to apportion blame, we believe that the panels' effectiveness has been hampered over the years by the unavailability of a sympathetic framework to facilitate understanding of the interpersonal factors contributing to the tragedy.[52]

Thus, they ask not just 'What happened?' but 'How can those events be understood?'

Reder *et al.* optimistically believe that we may be moving towards a less blaming approach, by employing an inquisitorial rather than adversarial setting. Although it might be argued by those who emphasise the procedural advantages of an adversarial setting that the inquisitorial approach actually facilitates rather than obviates finger-pointing, involvement with the Inquiry process and the inevitable delay before its conclusions are made public, may help to prepare those who are to be criticised. As Martin suggested

> The trauma of hearings, followed by the wait for results may be unnerving, but it gives time for people to reflect and prepare their rationalizations for the outcome.[53]

Of course, not all inquiries entail live hearings. Some child abuse inquiries have followed the model of written reports being submitted to the panel who then analyse them. This leads to participants in an incident being required to re-construct events in writing – possibly or even probably selectively – for the inquiry panel to deconstruct. This model is currently followed by the ACPC (Area Child Protection Committee). The alternative model is to call witness evidence live, but this then creates an arguably greater necessity for representation. And may require, as in the Scott Inquiry, participants to comment on a draft report to avoid errors of fact.

That the live hearing is a powerful forum for blaming and shaming is self-evident. What may be less evident is that the process of the Inquiry, which commences long before the hearing and extends after the publication of the report, is also a socially constructed process. Commenting on the original scandal, Sherman has observed

> scandals do not just happen: they are socially constructed phenomena involving the co-operation and conflict of many people.[54]

But these observations are equally apt for the process of the Inquiry. Although there will be broad terms of reference, how the Inquiry seeks to fulfil its role will be socially determined. The questions it asks, the problems it perceives or fails to perceive, the resolution of which participants are to be seen as having fallen from grace, will be a reflection of the make-up of the panel, no matter how skilled they are at remaining objective. Their preconceptions and the very experience which selects them for the task, will influence how that task is performed.

To illustrate, a determination of professional negligence would require that the relevant professional be found to have fallen below a reasonable standard of care. What that standard is varies, but by reference to medical negligence, the court would have to ask itself whether any substantial body of responsible opinion within a given specialism would support the care provided as acceptable. Thus, the standard to be attained is set by the relevant professional body – even if only a small number of the relevant speciality support a particular practice (or omission) – although the judgement as to whether there is sufficient evidence to sustain that finding lies with the court.[55] At an Inquiry the relevant professional expertise is often to be found imbued in the various members of the Inquiry; for example, the Jason Mitchell Inquiry benefited from the participation of a consultant forensic psychiatrist with a joint academic post; a former Director of Social Services; a former Deputy Assistant Commissioner from the Metropolitan Police with ongoing experience at the Mental Health Act Commission as the Commissioner for Complaints; and a clinical psychologist – also a former member of the Mental Health Act Commission. Together with the distinguished chairmanship of Sir Louis Blom-Cooper QC, they formed a formidable body of expert opinion. Their views will inevitably have suffused the judgements they reached.

However, this can lead to its own problems, as each professional member may be tempted to judge not only according to his or her own professional standards, but also on the basis of his or her own experience.

To illustrate from an earlier Inquiry – that of Maria Colwell, published in 1974.[56] The three-member Inquiry Panel were unable to agree on a final report and a minority report in relation to the interpretation of the facts and the emphasis that should be given to them was submitted by Olive Stevenson. Her observations, in paragraph 247, are worth reporting in detail for their perspicacity:

> As a social worker, my education and experience has taught me that in such matters, there is no one truth; in considering the subtleties of human emotions everyone is subjective. One's feeling, attitudes and experience colour one's perceptions. This is as true for me as it is for my colleagues. And, when one is dealing with events now some time in the past, drawing to a large extent on records for evidence, and inevitably affected by the eventual tragedy, the probability of distortion in interpretation is all the greater.

Her minority report concluded that her fellow members of the Inquiry had not done justice to the difficulties inherited by the relevant social worker and her colleagues.

Decision-making by groups – whether they be tribunals, inquiries, juries or benches of magistrates, is predicated on the notion that their decisions will somehow be better – perhaps better informed, fairer or whatever – than those of single decision-makers. This notion may be not only misleading, but simply wrong – in that group decisions may be both more extreme than can be justified or based on presumptions of expertise which are undermined rather than enhanced by the group context. This is not the place for a comprehensive analysis of these arguments; suffice it to say that the combination of an inquisitorial method which draws on the expertise of panel members and places it into a group context may be an explosive combination.[57]

Stephen Sedley, in his centenary address to the LSE, explicitly recognised the dilemma for adjudicators – of the tension between the need for detachment and the need for that detachment to be properly diluted by involvement.[58] If no judge comes to the adjudicative process free of preconceptions, how much more difficult must it be for those involved in an inquisitorial process where their very selection is based on the relevance of their expertise? How this comes into play is not only moderated by the role of the counsel to the Inquiry and the Inquiry's support team, but also by the way in which the Inquiry frames and interprets its own terms of reference. To illustrate, the Jason Mitchell Inquiry was charged with looking at the quality of care and control he received 'in the years and months leading up to his absence on December 9th 1994'. But how far back were they expected to go? Notably, this Inquiry had to adjourn rather than close the hearing on what was supposed to be its last day when the diligence of one of its support staff threw up documentation that potentially cast completely new light on the case. Yet this documentation, unknown to many of those responsible for Jason Mitchell's care during the period the Inquiry had chosen to address, predated his index offence in 1990 by several years. Its perceived relevance goes both to the question of 'Should it have been known?' and 'What difference would it have made had it been known?' The answers will depend on the perspective that psychologists, psychiatrists and lawyers, to name but three, have on the philosophical debate about the precursors of behaviour. Whether, to what extent and how Inquiries should be exploring issues of causation are addressed by both David Carson and Nigel Eastman in their chapters in this book.

(d) Catharsis

The Victim's Charter, which sets out the rights of victims of crime, states that 'Everything will be done to avoid distress to victims or their relatives'.[59] It is self-evident that an Inquiry will have a major impact on secondary victims; not only can the Inquiry aid 'fact-finding', a role for which the secondary victims would otherwise have to look to the Health Services Ombudsman, but the very process may be cathartic.

The Department of Health, which advises on the setting-up of these Inquiries, is mindful of the impact they can have on relatives. It advocates that relatives (of both victim and perpetrator) be kept well informed – both before the Inquiry starts and prior to the publication of the report. It also recommends that these participants should be the first to give evidence to the Inquiry.

This role for relatives is somewhat at odds with the strong preference within the Department of Health for private Inquiries. Indeed, subsection iii above of the NHS Guidance, which makes plain that the final report need not necessarily be made public provided its 'main findings' are made available to 'interested parties', rather begs the question as to the definition of interested parties at a private hearing and does nothing properly to protect the already ambivalent role of secondary victims at Inquiries.[60]

Summary

An 'Inquiry after Homicide' is a mixed blessing. Although in the immediate aftermath of a tragedy there may be an overriding sense that it is necessary to 'get at the truth' of what happened, it is evident that this objective can only be approached at considerable expense to both people and resources.[61] Indeed, in order to provide some limited protection to the basic rights of individuals subjected to the investigation it is probably necessary to undermine the advantages of an inquisitorial approach with procedural safeguards. These, in turn, can augment an already protracted and painful process.

There is a clear temptation to argue that we appoint to Inquiries people of such calibre and experience that they can be trusted to protect the interests of and deal fairly with those involved. This may well be true. But it leaves unresolved the problematic position of those awaiting and undergoing the process, detriment to whom can only be weighed against the effectiveness of the Inquiry's conclusions and recommendations. As Kennedy noted, the Ritchie Inquiry was widely regarded as having made sensible recommendations which were welcomed by mental health professionals. Indeed, his view is that there may be little new to say in this area. But the Report's recommendations remain to be accepted by Government.[62] What price the 'Inquiry after Homicide'?

Preliminary questions posed at the one-day seminar

(1) What role or roles do 'Inquiries after Homicide' play?

(2) What is the rationale for holding inquiries into homicides by persons with some connection with the mental health services, but not into homicides committed by other identifiable groups; for example, life licence prisoners, those on parole or probation orders, or those who have a record of violence, but no current contact with the criminal justice system?

(3) What are the consequences of the purchaser/provider split? If Inquiries only have to be independent of the provider could internal inquiries launched by the purchaser suffice?

(4) Can we afford the exponential growth of multi-million pound inquiries? What are the true human and financial costs of Inquiries? Should we take account of costs beyond those to the purchaser (which can run to £250,000 per inquiry) to include some of the hidden costs? For example, for representation of witnesses; lost opportunity costs (on what else might this money have been profitably spent?); any resulting paralysis or defensive practices.

(5) Is 'mopping up' cost-efficient? Should we be actively exploring preventive or ameliorative measures? Is it possible that Inquiries may do more good than harm (other than for lawyers!)? Are there lessons to be learnt for achieving good practice, not merely avoiding bad practice? By analogy with research on violence and mental disorder, should we focus more closely on models of well-being – where violence decreases after certain interventions – rather than focusing our Inquiries on cases where things go wrong?

(6) As Rhys Davies has asked 'What … is the relationship between scandal, inquiry and real improvement in services? Is there a direct causal link, a tortuous one or do inquiries provide employment for lawyers, doctors and others, to no great effect?'[63]

(7) Are Inquiries playing an increasingly influential role in the

evolution of Mental Health Law in England and Wales? Has
the plethora of recommendations had any impact? Should it
have done?

(8) What happens to recommendations? Why do some recommendations get taken up, others ignored and some constructed from the ambience of a report? Does an Inquiry
report primarily provide opportunities for agenda setting
and campaigning rather than a considered basis for legislative reform?

(9) Do Inquiries have any legitimate continuing role where their
recommendations are not implemented, or are implemented
selectively? Should there be some mechanism for Inquiries
to follow-up or monitor enforcement of their recommendations – or are they just a 'flash in the pan' designed to
assuage public concern?

(10) Inquiries generate considerable media interest, which can
be beneficial where this draws attention to and remedies
deficiencies in resources. But does such coverage also alien-
ate the public further from mentally disordered offenders,
making their re-integration into the community more problematic? Does media presentation also add to the anticipa-
tory and actual stress experienced by witnesses at Inquiries?

(11) Are there tangible benefits for secondary victims? What is
the role of the Inquiry for victims' families? What do victims'
families and friends need? Do they principally need control,
information, expiation, apologies, or what? Do they need to
be reassured that lessons have been learnt?

(12) Do/should secondary victims have a role; should the 'public
interest' be satiated? Should some procedural safeguards be
forgone to facilitate the 'public interest' in the search for
truth?

(13) Why are some reports confidential? Who are the 'interested
parties' if an Inquiry Report is not to be made public?

(14) Is dissipating social anxiety by attributing blame too un-
equal an exchange? Can Inquiries have unintended consequences? For example, comment in the *Guardian* within one
editorial shifted from 'the Rous case is not an indictment of
community care in principle' (echoing the view of the Inquiry
Report that the problems stemmed largely from the stand-

ard and regulation of community care) to 'In the wake of such high profile, emotive and tragic incidents, public confidence in the whole future of community care needs to be restored'. (15) Does the Inquiry process inevitably attribute blame? What steps might be taken to encourage Inquiries to stand-back from the detail of the particular case under consideration?

Notes

1. Department of Health (1994) *Guidance on the discharge of mentally disordered people and their continuing care in the community* NHS Executive HSG(94)27 and LASSL(94)4, 10 May 1994. See also Appendix A where selected sections are reproduced in full.

2. The Guidance qualifies this requirement by noting in the same paragraph that 'The only exception is where the victim is a child and it is considered that the report by the Area Protection Committee ... fully covers the remit of an independent inquiry...'.

3. Of 22 cases of homicide *reviewed* by the Boyd Report as having been committed by persons who had had contact with the psychiatric services in the preceding twelve months, fifteen were male and seven female; Boyd W.D. (1994) *A Preliminary Report on Homicide*, Steering Committee of the Confidential Inquiry into Homicides and Suicides by Mentally Ill People. Two features are notable. First, the differential diagnoses; young women are more likely to have been suffering from depression and to have killed their children, while young men in the group disproportionately suffered from a schizophrenic illness. Secondly, there are proportionately more women amongst the group than would be expected given that women are, on average, responsible for only 12 per cent of the annual homicide rate.

4. The hearing of Jason Mitchell's plea to triple manslaughter on 7 July 1995 at Ipswich Crown Court took less than half a day, even though two psychiatrists were called to give evidence by the defence in mitigation.

5. A list of reported, ongoing and potential 'Inquiries after Homicide' appears in Appendix B.

6. Boyd (1994) op. cit., at 13.

7. Kennedy H. (1995) 'What is forensic psychiatry?', Paper presented to the joint Legal Action/Doughty Street Chambers conference on Mentally Disordered Defendants, 21 October 1995, London. The Boyd Report (1994) op. cit., at 10, notes that something over 100 persons each year are admitted to psychiatric care, either with or without a restriction on discharge, following homicide.

8. Multiple domestic homicides, for example, where a parent kills both spouse and children in one incident, are not uncommonly associated with depression – and depression which may previously not have been formally diagnosed in the perpetrator.

9. See also Appendix A. Further confusion arises as the title of the Department of Health Guidance refers to the generic 'mentally disordered people' and makes plain it is using the terminology of the *Mental Health Act 1983*. Similarly, the accompanying NHS Executive Summary makes reference to 'all patients who are discharged following referral to the specialist mental health services'. However, the preamble to the main Department of Health Guidance makes reference to 'mentally ill people in the community' in the context of discharge from hospital, and the Local Authority Social Services Letter refers in its paragraph 1 to 'mentally ill people who have been in contact with the specialist mental health services'. Accordingly, how wide the scope of mandatory Inquiries is intended to be, may be ambiguous to those unfamiliar with the finer distinctions of definition. Should an Inquiry follow a homicide committed by someone suffering from psychopathic disorder who has had contact with the psychiatric services perhaps in a prison setting? Where there has been no local authority or health service care, probably not, but it is a moot point.

10. Wade H.W.R. and Forsyth C.F. (1994) *Administrative Law*, 7th ed., Oxford, Clarendon Press.

11. Wraith R.E. and Lamb G.B. (1971) *Public Inquiries as an Instrument of Government*, London, George Allen and Unwin.

12. Wade and Forsyth (1994) op. cit., at 910.

13. Wraith and Lamb (1971) op. cit., at 14.

14. Segal Z. (1984) 'Tribunals of Inquiry: a British invention ignored in Britain', *Public Law*, 206-14 at 206.

15. Wraith and Lamb (1971) op. cit., at 212.

16. Ibid., at 212.

17. Royal Commission on Tribunals of Inquiry (Chairman: Salmon L.J.) (1966) Cmnd 3121, at 44.

18. Ibid., at 17-18

19. It is perhaps regrettable that there has been partial reliance on Salmon without either fully implementing or fully obviating the need for the criteria. Thus, the Report of the Learmont Inquiry (General Sir John Learmont KCB, CBE (1995) *Review of Prison Security in England and Wales* Cm 3020) discloses that guarantees of confidentiality and anonymity were given. But, the Inquiry then encountered difficulties where, having circulated elements of the draft report for comment to those subject to criticism, it considered itself unable to provide details of the basis and source of those criticisms (see paras 1.24-1.25).

20. Wraith and Lamb (1971) op. cit., at 213.

21. Ibid., at 215.

22. Sir Richard Scott (1995) 'Procedures at inquiries – the duty to be fair', *Law Quarterly Review*, 596-616

23. In a written parliamentary answer (4 December 1995) the Prime Minister said that £750,790 had been spent to date on 'external advice' relating to the inquiry (private lawyers for ministers, ex-ministers and civil servants) while the Treasury Solicitor's Department had charged £306,320 for legal services to Whitehall departments (see *Guardian*, 5 December 1995).

24. For a critique of investigative inquiries in the commercial arena see Graham C. and Riley C. (1996) 'Inquiries, company investigations and *Fayed v UK*', *European Public Law* (forthcoming). They similarly call for the development of a range of principles and rules to 'balance the needs of the individual with the requirements of an effective inquiry'.

25. House of Lords 16 February 1994 *Hansard* Vol. 552 No. 41 at Col. 208-10.

26. Ibid., at Col. 230-1.

27. The hospital inquiries were held under s.70 of the *National Health Service Act 1946* (which became s.84 of the 1977 Act). Section 84(1) states:

The Secretary of State may cause an inquiry to be held in any case where he deems it advisable to do so in connection with any matter arising under this Act.

The Inquiries enjoyed powers to compel witnesses to give evidence and produce documentation, with the sanction of criminal proceedings for recalcitrants. Although not so required, the Inquiries invariably were held in public.

Although the child abuse inquiries were non-statutory their *modus operandi* was not dissimilar to the hospital inquiries – hearing oral evidence in public and securing all relevant written documentation. It should be stressed that where co-operation is forthcoming, the difference between statutory and non-statutory hearings may be a canard. For as the Maria Colwell Report notes: 'Although we had no power to compel .... It is right to record that all the agencies concerned were entirely co-operative and made available for use all their relevant records', *Report of the Committee of Inquiry into the Care and Supervision Provided in Relation to Maria Colwell* (1974) DHSS, HMSO, at para 5.

28. Martin J.P. (1984) *Hospitals in Trouble*, Oxford, Blackwell.

29. Reder P., Duncan S. and Gray M. (1993) *Beyond Blame: Child Abuse Tragedies Revisited*, London, Routledge. See also Department of Health and Social Security (1982) *Child Abuse: A Study of Inquiry Reports 1973-1981*, London, HMSO, and Department of Health (1991) *Child Abuse: A Study of Inquiry Reports 1980-1989*, London, HMSO.

30. Mr and Mrs Wilson were a retired couple living in the same vicinity as Robert Mitchell, Jason Mitchell's father. The majority of victims killed by those suffering from mental disorder are, like the victims of 'mentally ordered' offenders, either family members or known to the perpetrator. Where perpetrators kill a member of their own family, as did Jason Mitchell, the surviving family members suffer an acute double loss. Notably, of the 22 cases reviewed by the Boyd

Report, (1994) op. cit., at 17, only two of the victims were strangers to the perpetrators.

31. Peay J. (1989) *Tribunals on Trial: A Study of Decision-Making Under the Mental Health Act 1983*, Oxford, Clarendon Press.

32. See Link B.G., Andrews H. and Cullen F.T. (1992) 'The violent and illegal behaviour of mental patients reconsidered', *American Sociological Review* 57, 275-92; Mulvey E.P. (1994) 'Assessing the evidence of a link between mental illness and violence', *Hospital and Community Psychiatry* 45, 663-8; and Swanson J.W., Holzer C.E., Ganju V.K. and Jono R.T. (1990) 'Violence and psychiatric disorder in the community: evidence from the epidemiological catchment area surveys', *Hospital and Community Psychiatry* 41, 761-70.

33. See generally the work of John Monahan and his team for the MacArthur Foundation in the United States.

34. The worst risk group of all are those suffering serious mental illness who abuse alcohol and drugs, where 66 per cent of those questioned in self-report studies had been involved in serious incidents of violence.

35. In particular, the Ben Silcock incident. While suffering from schizophrenia, Mr Silcock climbed into the lions' den at London Zoo and was mauled. The incident was captured on camera.

36. Martin (1984) op. cit., at 69.

37. For example, the Inquiry chaired by Nicola Davies QC found that one of the occasions on which the 'chain of causation' which led to the death of Jonathan Newby might have been broken was the failure of a telephone operator to respond appropriately to an abusive 999 call. See Davies N. (1995) *Report of the Jonathan Newby Inquiry*, Oxford, July 1995, at 141-2.

38. Blom-Cooper L., Hally H. and Murphy E. (1995) *The Falling Shadow: One Patient's Mental Health Care 1978-1993*, Duckworth. Georgina, an occupational therapist, was killed by Andrew Robinson, while he was an in-patient at the hospital where she was working.

39. Woodley L., Dixon K., Lindow V., Oyebode O., Sandford T. and Simblet S. (1995) *The Woodley Team Report: Report of the independent review panel to the East London and the City Health Authority and Newham Council, following a homicide in July 1994 by a person suffering with a severe mental illness*, London, East London and the City Health Authority. See also *Guardian*, 26 September 1995.

40. Martin (1984) op. cit., at 97.

41. Ritchie J., Dick D. and Lingham R. (1994) *The Report of the Inquiry into the Care and Treatment of Christopher Clunis*, presented to the North East Thames and South East Thames Health Authorities, London, HMSO, at para 2.1.5.

42. Sir Louis Blom-Cooper QC (1993) 'Public inquiries' in M. Freeman and B. Hepple (eds) *Current Legal Problems Vol. 46 Part II Collected Papers*, Oxford University Press, at 206.

43. Ibid., at 206.

44. Ibid., at 205.

45. Sir Richard Scott (1995) op. cit., at 614-15.

46. Blom-Cooper (1993) op. cit., at 205.

47. British Association of Social Workers, *The Social Worker as Appropriate Adult under the Police and Criminal Evidence Act 1984*, Birmingham. The code advises breach in such situations.

48. Palmer C. (1995) 'The effectiveness of the safeguards in PACE for mentally disordered and mentally handicapped suspects – a South Yorkshire study', paper presented to the LAG/Doughty Street Chambers Conference on Mentally Disordered Defendants, 21 October 1995, London.

49. Robertson T. (1992) 'The Romans were right', paper delivered in Sydney to the Seminar on Advanced Criminal Law, 14 November 1992, at 3. The paper examines the role of tribunals held under the *Independent Commission Against Corruption Act 1988*. These are supposedly engaged in the investigatory process as to whether to institute criminal proceedings but, in Robertson's view, actually pre-judge guilt and then punish through shaming and social control.

50. Ibid., at 11-12.

51. Reder, Duncan and Gray (1993) op. cit., at 135.

52. Ibid., at 135.

53. Martin (1984) op. cit., at 67.

54. Sherman L.W. (1978) *Scandal and Reform: Controlling Police Corruption*, Berkeley, University of California Press, at 59, cited in Robertson (1992) op. cit.

55. *Bolam v Friern Hospital Management Committee* [1957] 1 WLR 582; see also the Court of Appeal in *Defreitas v O'Brien & Another* (1995) *The Times*, 16 February.

56. DHSS (1974) *Report of the Committee of Inquiry into the Care and Supervision Provided in Relation to Maria Colwell*, London, HMSO.

57. See, for example, Peay J. (1981) 'Mental Health Review Tribunals: just or efficacious safeguards?', *Law and Human Behavior* 5, 2/3 161-86.

58. Sedley S. (1995) 'Autonomy and the rule of law'. Centenary Address to the London School of Economics, 23 October 1995.

59. Home Office (1990) *Victim's Charter. A Statement of the Rights of Victims of Crime*, at 20-1.

60. Now partially revised by *Building Bridges* (para 5.1.19) – see the discussion by Crichton and Sheppard in this book.

61. Quantifying the true financial cost of an Inquiry proved an impossible task. Although the immediate cost to the Purchasing Authority can be estimated – with some Inquiries totalling over £250,000 – there are other less obvious costs. For example, the Jason Mitchell Inquiry learnt from the Medical Protection Society of some of the costs in cases in which their members had been involved; disbursements, experts' fees and counsel's fees on occasions totalled over

£100,000 (excluding solicitors' costs). And, as the MPS observed, 'the costs do not of course give any indication of the emotional and mental trauma for the practitioner, and indeed his colleagues'. These sums could relate to the representation of only one doctor; at the Jason Mitchell Inquiry, three 'parties' at the hearing were separately represented. Hence, the true financial cost, whatever it may be, is likely to be substantial.

62. Kennedy H. (1995) op. cit.

63. Davies R. (1995) 'Inquiry into inquiries', *Open Mind* 75 at 6-8.

Inquiries into Homicide:
A Legal Perspective

Oliver Thorold and John Trotter

The NHS Guidelines

1. The process of inquiring into homicides by patients, previously discretionary, was mandated by NHS Executive Guidelines dated 10 May 1994 (NHS Executive HSG (94)27). The key section of the Guidance is set out in Appendix A. Notably, the procedure for inquiry panels is not prescribed, and inquiries frequently reveal significant variations of approach.

The power to set up a statutory inquiry

2. Inquiries launched pursuant to the May 1994 NHS Executive Guidance have so far, it is believed, all been non-statutory. The statutory provisions have not therefore been invoked. It will be argued in this chapter that difficulties encountered by non-statutory inquiries in obtaining documentary evidence, or compelling witnesses, might well create a need to turn a non-statutory inquiry into a statutory one, even if this has not yet occurred.

3. Where a statutory inquiry is established, whether under Section 125 of the Mental Health Act 1983 or any other power, the inquiry is normally equipped with the powers set out in Section 250 of the Local Government Act 1972. These powers enable the 'person appointed' to require any person to attend to give evidence or to produce any documents in his custody or

control. There is also a power to take evidence on oath, though this is in no way mandated (Section 250(2)).

4. The Minister can order that any costs incurred be paid by the local authority, and costs orders can be made against parties (Section 250(4).

5. Apart from power to compel a witness and obtain documents, statutory status has comparatively minor implications. In neither form of inquiry is it mandatory to administer the oath, and many statutory inquiries do not. Costs orders against parties are not normally a feature of the inquiry process, save when a party resorts to judicial review, or other legal proceedings. Principles of fairness and natural justice are applicable alike. A duty to forewarn of possible criticism is borne by any inquiry.

6. The nature of the inquiry, of either type, was considered by Kennedy J (as he then was) in *R v. Secretary of State for Health, ex parte Prison Officers Association* [1992] Crown Office Digest 177, an attempt to judicially review the decision to set up the Ashworth Inquiry, under Sir Louis Blom-Cooper's chairmanship:

> It is important to bear in mind that this inquiry, whether with or without statutory powers, is like others that have gone before it – for example, Lord Scarman's Red Lion Square statutory inquiry and the non-statutory Strangeways inquiry conducted by Woolf LJ – just an inquiry. It is by nature inquisitorial, not adversarial. No one is on trial even if at times certain individuals feel tempted to suggest otherwise. So decisions such as which documents are seen, which witnesses are called and how the witnesses are handled in terms of how much evidence is led, what cross-examination is allowed and to what extent attention is paid to rules governing the admissibility of evidence are all matters for the Committee subject only to the overriding requirement that the proceedings shall be fair.

Appointment

7. The first practical step is usually to locate a suitable Chair, traditionally a lawyer, and in consultation with the Chair to identify other suitable members of the panel. It is virtually

inevitable that a psychiatrist will be needed if the patient was under psychiatric care, and a third member is frequently drawn from those with social work expertise. The explicit reference to 'social care needs' in the Guidance will usually make such an appointment appropriate. While a panel of three is common, the issues raised may suggest a larger number. It may well be, for example, appropriate to empanel a psychologist.

8. The process of identifying panel members will normally need to be undertaken shortly after the criminal event, and almost certainly before the criminal process has taken its course. The reference in the Guidance to the holding of an inquiry 'after the completion of any legal proceedings' reflects a proper caution about the risk of prejudicing a criminal trial.

Public/private

9. At an early stage the sponsoring authority will need to decide whether the inquiry should be public or private. This is not quite as clear-cut a decision as it may sound, because an inquiry initially conceived of as being public may decide to hear certain witnesses in private. A mixture of approaches is perfectly feasible, and quite common. Statutory and non-statutory inquiries can both be held in private or in public.

10. A decision to hold an inquiry in private greatly limits the role of legal representatives. Indeed the question of which witnesses ought or ought not to have legal representation is effectively avoided. There is obviously no opportunity for representatives to question other witnesses.

11. If the evidence is given in private the inquiry panel will have to consider how far they should communicate evidence of witnesses to other witnesses. Principles of natural justice would require that any criticism which the panel intend to take into account should be communicated to the party affected.

Obtaining documents

12. Obtaining the requisite documentation will inevitably be the first organisational step facing any inquiry. If the sponsoring authority can itself supply the entire documentation, the inquiry's task is made much easier. But this will be rare. More commonly the patient may have received care from, or crossed the jurisdictional boundaries of, health authorities, general practitioners, the special hospital system, social work departments, the prison service, and probation departments. While key reports and discharge summaries may have travelled with the patient, no inquiry which sets itself appropriate goals of thoroughness can readily assume that such summaries are sufficient. Assessment of the adequacy of communication between different agencies over time is almost inevitably an issue which the inquiry has to address.

13. Unless the Department of Health equips an inquiry with statutory powers, it is difficult, if not impossible, to obtain all relevant documents without obtaining the patient's agreement. Agencies other than the sponsoring authority frequently condition release of documents on the patient's formal written consent. Individual doctors risk disciplinary proceedings before the General Medical Council if the patient does not release them from their obligation of confidence.

14. Perhaps surprisingly, the patient, or where the patient has died, his/her relatives, can usually be persuaded to co-operate. If the violent event has led to criminal proceedings the support of the patient's defence lawyers can often be crucial. They may have secured a trusting relationship with the patient. If they can be persuaded to advise the patient to co-operate, the necessary consent can more readily be obtained

15. If the violent event occurred when the patient was unmedicated, and medication is restored after arrest, the patient's attitude to the prospect of an inquiry may change over time. There are therefore delicate issues of timing involved in making the approach. The importance of success is critical. Delay in

obtaining consent will delay the assembly of documents, and without the documents the inquiry will be unable to see with clarity what the key issues are.

16. Although no inquiry, so far, has reported that it was unable to discharge its terms of reference by reason of inability to obtain crucial documents or evidence, it is quite possible to imagine that this could happen. A refusal by the patient to give consent, or, equally problematic, a revocation by the patient of consent previously given, could place an inquiry in grave difficulties. A decision to equip the inquiry with statutory powers could then be unavoidable.

Confidentiality and disclosure

17. The consent of the subject removes any barrier to disclosure based upon principles of confidentiality. That is explicitly recognised, for example, in the Department of Health's 1988 Guidance 'Personal Social Services: Confidentiality of Personal Information' (LAC(88)17, HN(88)24, HN(FP)(88)22):

> Nothing in this guidance prevents the disclosure of personal information for whatever purpose with the consent, expressly or by necessary implication, of the subject.

The Guidance recognises that for the consent of a mentally ill or mentally handicapped person to be valid, he must be capable of managing his own affairs (para. 45). If the patient is subject to the Court of Protection, or if there is an Attorney with an Enduring Power, their interests must be taken into account. In other cases consent may be validly obtained through an agent.

18. The same principle would apply with respect to a medical obligation of confidence. Lawyer client privilege, which vests in the client and not the lawyer, can likewise be waived by the patient/client, and in those circumstances documents otherwise falling within the scope of the privilege can be obtained. Indeed, more generally, it can be suggested that the patient's consent should be sufficient to obtain disclosure to an inquiry of records

from any agency, subject only to valid resistance on grounds of public interest immunity.

19. The medical records on a patient held by the sponsoring authority are, in principle, subject to an obligation of confidence. However, it is submitted that they may be disclosed without the patient's consent on two bases: first, to enable the authority the better to perform its own statutory function, and secondly in the public interest. The public interest is always capable of justifying or excusing, or even mandating, disclosure of confidential material.

20. Disclosure of documents without the consent of the subject is far more problematic. For example, the Department of Health Guidance mentioned above cites only two justifications, for 'social work purposes' or 'in strictly limited and exceptional cases, where the law or the public interest may override the subject's right to confidentiality' (para 16). Under the former, in the context of a department or another organisation discharging its statutory function, the Guidance says disclosure can be made where a 'committee of inquiry may need to have personal information in considering a case'. Under the latter there is, perhaps regrettably, no explicit reference to disclosure to an inquiry of the kind under consideration. Although this can be read as permitting disclosure, this is not the invariable interpretation placed on the Guidance by authorities and departments. Greater clarity and explicitness would undoubtedly be welcome.

21. Guidance to doctors from the General Medical Council does not at present enunciate in clear terms any right or duty to breach confidence in the cause of co-operating with an inquiry. The only exception to the obligation of confidence to which the inquiry can point is contained in Rule 81(g) of the GMC's 'Blue Book' on Professional Conduct and Discipline, that the public interest 'might override the doctor's duty to maintain confidentiality'. Yet for the doctor concerned the choice is unenviable. Faced with a complaint to the GMC from his erstwhile patient, he/she might be able to persuade the Council that Rule 81(g) was in point, but there appears to be no precedent to reassure.

Moreover there is no system whereby the doctor can obtain an advisory ruling. After consultation with his medical defence society a general practitioner approached by the Torbay Inquiry declined to take the risk.

22. If it is desired that inquiries should continue to be set up on a non-statutory basis, we see advantage in clarifying circular guidance to ensure that co-operation and disclosure is explicitly stated to be proper. It might also assist if the GMC and UKCC, and any other professional bodies, were asked to clarify their disciplinary codes, stating whether the giving of evidence to a public inquiry constitutes grounds for overriding confidentiality.

The power to require evidence

23. In the absence of statutory powers, inquiries are largely dependent upon good will and a sense of duty for obtaining the attendance of witnesses. Many contracts of employment within the public service stipulate that the employee should co-operate with any independent inquiry. Consequently those still in the employ of the sponsoring authority will normally be obliged to give evidence if called. Ex-employees by contrast can refuse without risk of sanction.

24. Professional bodies, such as the GMC or the UKCC, would not regard a failure to give evidence to an inquiry as sufficiently serious to warrant disciplinary sanction.

25. Is there any power available to a non-statutory inquiry to require documentary evidence to be produced? Even the suggestion may be something of a surprise. Under Order 38, rule 19 of the Rules of the Supreme Court states that a writ of *subpoena ad testificandum* or *duces tecum* may be issued to 'an inferior court or tribunal'. The editors of the White Book, citing *Currie v. Chief Constable of Surrey* [1982] 1 All ER 89, suggest that to qualify the inferior tribunal must be:

(1) recognised by law
(2) acting judicially or quasi-judicially
(3) acting upon evidence, although that evidence need not be on oath, and
(4) the tribunal must have insufficient power on its own to compel the attendance of witnesses or the production of documents.

26. A non-statutory inquiry obviously fulfils the third and fourth requirements, but what about the first two? In *Currie*, a case involving a police disciplinary hearing, McNeill J held that to be 'recognised by law' a tribunal need not be statutory. Support for both the proposition that the inquiry is legally recognised, and the requirement that the tribunal be acting quasi-judicially (it is clearly not acting judicially), could be found from the fact that the inquiry is susceptible to judicial review. A non-statutory inquiry established by a health authority is probably so susceptible, though we are unaware of any case which explicitly so finds.

27. While the matter is uncertain, it appears distinctly arguable. So far as we are aware, no non-statutory inquiry has yet attempted to obtain a subpoena under this rule.

Procedure

28. Although the May 1994 Guidance refers to an inquiry being held 'after any legal proceedings', preparation, particularly assembly of documents, needs to be well under way before any trial is complete.

29. A principal determinant of procedure is likely to be whether the inquiry is to be conducted in public or private. If in public, there is clear merit in a preliminary meeting, at which the terms of reference can be announced, any applications for representation can be made and adjudicated, and the procedure to be followed can be specified. There is no particular reason why the preliminary meeting need await the conclusion of the legal proceedings. No evidence will be called.

30. The essential legal proposition is that inquiry procedure is a matter for the discretion of the panel itself, who alone decide how their inquiry should proceed. Within that discretion, however, decisions made on legal representation should perhaps be referable to a principle. Sir Louis Blom-Cooper, in the Torbay Inquiry and the Jason Mitchell Inquiry, stated that legal representation 'would be granted strictly on the basis that the party needs to protect some right or interest which may be thought reasonably to be in jeopardy or subject to potential criticism'.

31. Applying that principle, representation would normally be granted to those bearing clinical or other responsibility shortly before the criminal event, or possibly earlier. An application made on behalf of Jason Mitchell himself to be represented was refused, on the grounds that though he had an interest in the inquiry, he was in not in any real sense liable to criticism, and he could submit any evidence he wished. In recent inquiries Sir Louis has always made clear that representation does not carry any automatic right to question witnesses, 'cross-examination' being at the discretion of the panel.

32. Only rarely will inquiries fund representation. Parties will usually be reliant on their own methods of finance.

33. Such issues are unlikely to arise at all if the inquiry is held in private. Witnesses will not be able to attend sessions where others give evidence, and though they may be notified of any criticism, they would not themselves, or through representatives, be able to put questions to them.

34. The use of 'counsel to the inquiry' has found increasing favour in recent times. The principal merit lies in the opportunity to incorporate the different interests of a number of panel members into a single sequence of questions. It may also be easier to reflect on the quality and import of the evidence if one has the chance to listen to rather than to conduct the questioning process.

35. Where the inquiry is public numerous procedural issues

arise, which perhaps should be regarded more as questions of management than law. Thus decisions need to be made on:

(1) the extent to which medical records are copied to participants, the restrictions placed on their use, and their return,

(2) when witnesses provide statements, their availability to other participants and the press,

(3) whether a transcript will be available, undoubtedly a great advantage for those who cannot maintain continual attendance,

(4) whether expert evidence will be taken,

(5) whether participants will have an opportunity to make submissions at the close of the inquiry, and if so whether written or oral.

36. Perhaps the most important procedural issue concerns the extent to which participants will be warned of likely areas of criticism. The report of the Royal Commission on Tribunals of Inquiry 1966 – the Salmon Report – stated:

> Before any person who is involved in an inquiry is called as a witness, he should be informed of any allegations which are made against him and the substance of the evidence in support of them.

Even though the principle was enunciated with statutory inquiries in mind, it has come to be regarded as applicable to all. The purpose is plain and understandable. No witness should be in a position where he is ignorant of criticism made of him. Criticism can lead to public obloquy and a blighted career.

37. The application of the principle is not free from difficulty. Documents may be provided after evidence has begun. An inquiry may not appreciate the vulnerability of a witness to criticism before he/she gives evidence. Indeed the very process of giving evidence may reveal the vulnerability. In the Kimberley Carlile Inquiry two witnesses received Salmon letters after giving evidence, and their advocates left no doubt that they regarded this as very unfair. Clearly where witnesses are served with Salmon letters after giving evidence, they should have the opportunity to give further evidence.

38. The principle is a worthy one, but, it is submitted, cannot be converted into a rigid rule. The paramount duty of the inquiry is to inquire and report, faithful to the entirety of the evidence obtained.

39. There are, however, a number of lessons. First, great care must be taken to collect, read and understand all the relevant material at the earliest possible stage, again underlining the cardinal importance of obtaining documentary evidence quickly. Considerable care must be taken in drafting Salmon letters – there must be no room for misunderstanding what the area of potential criticism might be. Finally, it may be prudent to let the participants know that while every attempt will be made to avoid the late service of Salmon letters, it may prove to be unavoidable.

40. It is an extension of the same principle that on occasions inquiries have made available to parties affected sections of their draft report with critical passages. The person affected may then comment and seek to dissuade.

Conclusion

41. The inquiry process remains substantially free from legal technicality, with the benefit of judicial insistence on a wide margin of discretion vesting in the person(s) appointed. If inquiries are established without statutory powers, and the issues require access to disparate documentation, the speedy assembly of documents can be the most difficult issue they face. That difficulty can in turn delay a comprehensive understanding of the material, and threaten to undermine attempts to ensure that all participants are treated fairly, and forewarned of areas of vulnerability. It is suggested that there is no identifiable gain, and clear disadvantage, from denying inquiries statutory powers to require production of documents and the ability to compel witnesses.

4

Ruminations on Inquiries

Cecil Clothier

Every day, everywhere, someone is inquiring into a matter in
which things seem to have gone wrong. It may be a disappoint-
ing fall in turnover at some branch or in some division of an
enterprise, a disaster from apparently natural causes or seem-
ing misconduct on the part of a public service or officials thereof.
Quite often the subject matter of an inquiry involves the possibility that someone concerned in the affair may have committed
a serious crime, such as murder. There are almost as many ways
of conducting these inquiries as there are persons to hold them.

Every civil or criminal trial is in essence an inquiry into
disputed facts and an attempt to arrive at the truth. It is natural
that the procedures which have been developed and refined in
the courts over many years should have provided a fundamental
approach to the process of inquiry. However, the procedures of
inquiries outside the judicial system have always been more
flexible and less formal. But the fundamental principles of
natural justice must still be observed if the inquiry is to com-
mand assent for its conclusions and to avoid judicial review.

The public has a general but unspecific interest in seeing that
justice is done between citizens, so that by long tradition the
public is admitted to courts of law. Nevertheless, if privacy
seems to be more in the public interest than proceedings in
public, even a court of justice may be closed to the public by the
judge.

In the domain of inquiries into matters of public rather than
individual concern, criticisms have been made as to both the
methodology and the personalities involved. It almost goes without saying that the person selected to conduct any inquiry must

be as independent of the matters under scrutiny as it is possible to be for anyone living in a complex society. But we are all involved with one another and hold views about the propriety of each other's conduct which we carry with us into any activity in which we engage. Independence is always a relative, never an absolute, concept.

It has become customary to appoint an individual thought to be well qualified for the particular subject of the inquiry. The eminence of the person appointed varies with the degree of public anxiety which has been aroused. Thereafter the person conducting the inquiry is usually left to determine the procedure to be followed and whether the public interest would best be served by holding it in public or private. Lord Salmon laid down the principles of natural justice which have to be observed if the inquiry is to be acceptable both to the public and to the persons involved.

It is thus a fundamentally important decision to be made at the outset of any inquiry whether to hold it entirely in public, entirely in private, or partly in each. Whatever decision is made about this, it will not satisfy everyone. The media will always be in favour of a public inquiry, piously exclaiming that their sole purpose is to inform an anxious readership. But of course a public inquiry affords exciting copy and often ready-made headlines, sometimes for months on end.

The public attitude, on the other hand, is generally motivated by a proper and justifiable anger at events which seem as if they ought not to have happened. Regrettably this proper attitude declines all too often into a clamour for vengeance and scapegoats to be driven into the wilderness loaded with anger and guilt.

A tiresome cliché has been invented, namely, a 'full-public-inquiry', as if there were some sort of half-baked inquiry which might suffice on occasion. Many of those who use this expression have little idea of what they mean by it. Usually they are not thinking so much of arriving at the truth because they believe they have already got there. Rather they are hoping that someone or other close to the events in question, whom they often believe they have already identified, will have to appear publicly to be suitably chastised. But of course there are very many others who genuinely wish to see some fearful mishap carefully analysed and steps taken to minimise a recurrence, the only proper consideration.

Although it may sound rather hard, it must be remembered that it is not the sole, or even the main, purpose of an inquiry into disaster to offer solace to the victims. There are better ways of doing this. The report is not made to the victims but to those representatives of society who have the power to make things happen on behalf of us all. And the primary purpose of the inquiry, to my mind, is to enable society through its mechanisms to take whatever steps seem good to prevent a recurrence of some great disaster and its consequent suffering, not merely for the benefit of the victims (for whom it comes too late anyway) but for the future good of everyone. I believe that an inquiry is a learning tool and the allocation of blame is merely an incidental, if sometimes inevitable, side effect. The expiation of wrongdoing is for those agencies, including where appropriate the judicial system, wherein resides the power of retribution.

The truth, as always, comes off worst in these conflicts of purpose and interest. In public, it is almost impossible for anyone in the presence of colleagues at work, the national media, and a phalanx of lawyers eager to fault one's every utterance, to tell the truth, the whole truth and nothing but the truth. I believe that inquiries in public seldom, if ever, arrive at the innermost truth underlying the apparent miscarriage of some public affair. Which of us will go willingly into the witness-box to testify against our colleagues at work, unless we believe their conduct to have been downright criminal? But public inquiries may sometimes be a political necessity.

On the other hand, in the quiet atmosphere of a small and private room, with no more persons present than are necessary to conduct the inquiry and record the proceedings, the truth in my experience has a way of eventually coming to the surface, sometimes in a remarkable outburst of candour such as could never have been uttered at a public inquiry. But of course the public, ever devoted to the theory of conspiracy, mistrusts the outcome of such an inquiry because it cannot bring itself to forgo the delights of seeing some of those involved suffer public humiliation in cross-examination, nor bring itself to believe that those conducting such inquiries can be trusted to be both honest and competent in unearthing the facts. It follows that however they are done, few inquiries satisfy the persons principally involved.

Then there is the question of representation. At public inquiries there is usually a considerable band of lawyers representing various persons interested in the outcome. Though obvious, it perhaps needs to be said that the business of lawyers is to represent people and it would be unnatural for them not to support a proposal for a public inquiry. It has to be said also that professional representation not only slows the proceedings and increases the costs enormously, but in nearly all cases induces fear and apprehension in the lay witness.

In the case of inquiries in private, it is not, I think, usual to have representation of the parties. For my part, I invariably invite witnesses when writing to them to arrange their attendance to bring with them a friend, either family or union, but not a qualified advocate. This offer is surprisingly often declined, many witnesses feeling well able to deal with all questions put to them when they realise the nature of the proceedings.

The Parliamentary Commissioner for Administration (PCA) has evolved over the years since the office was instituted in 1967, an inquisitorial methodology which has by and large satisfied those complaining about maladministration by Departments of Government. Inquiries are conducted almost entirely in the privacy of the homes of complainants and witnesses, although occasionally there has been a formal hearing of evidence in the offices of the PCA. That this satisfies the majority of complainants is abundantly clear. Very many complainants begin their approach to the PCA by asking: 'Will I have to give evidence in public?' It is obvious from the circumstances in which the question is put, that if the answer were to be in the affirmative, the complaint would be forthwith abandoned. Moreover the public has little interest in the mismanagement of some individual's social security payments or income tax affairs. Such complaints are very numerous and seldom carry great implications for the public at large, unless the degree and frequency of mismanagement were to amount to a public scandal.

The PCA publishes an annual report on his work, giving anonymous accounts of some of his investigations. This report is examined by a Select Committee of Parliament, the proceedings of which are held in public and recorded and published. These arrangements seem reasonably well-adapted to the particular purposes of the PCA and I mention them only to show that there is no one way of conducting inquiries into miscarriages in public affairs and that for many purposes, an inquiry in private is preferred by very many citizens. But, of course, there are some mishaps so grievous, and arousing so much public outrage and concern, that nothing less than an inquiry in public would be politically acceptable.

In every inquiry, public or private, it is essential to protect witnesses from unfair attack or condemnation. In a public inquiry, confrontation is inevitable and witnesses are given at the inquiry itself an opportunity to defend themselves against attack by interested parties or their representatives. They may find it very difficult to do so. In an inquiry held in private, however, it is in the nature of the process that the witnesses do not confront each other, nor learn what others may be saying about them. Thus it has come about that the necessary protection is customarily provided by telling persons in advance that they are possible targets of criticism, and what are the issues which they must confront or on which the inquiry would like to hear from them. A record in writing is made of their evidence which is sent to them for editing (although their improvements on what they actually said are not always acceptable). However, they are not shown the actual record of the evidence of other witnesses. On occasion witnesses must be recalled to deal with some issue which has emerged in the course of the inquiry. This procedure tends to remove the elements of fear and emotion attendant upon a public inquiry and I truly believe arrives at conclusions nearer the truth of what happened than any other process. It certainly gives those persons within the range of criticism a good chance to defend themselves, unharassed by lawyers.

Very eminent persons have sometimes conducted inquiries

alone, usually in matters not calling for much technical knowledge of the subject. Such was the inquiry long ago by Lord Denning into the Profumo affair. It seems to me that it is increasingly difficult to satisfy public opinion in this way. The activities of people in all walks of life and the means by which they inform themselves in connection with their work have become so complex and so technical, that some acquaintance with the subject of the inquiry seems essential.

Certainly no sensible person should conduct an inquiry into a medical or aviation mishap, for example, without the assistance of two persons expert in the particular field of inquiry. The use of assessors in courts of justice has long been established, but there the judge remains the ultimate decider. It may be thought better nowadays when inquiring into a matter of public concern for the assessors to be equal partners in the making of the ultimate decisions, because this gives that much more weight to the outcome.

But I believe that a tribunal of more than three persons runs a variety of risks, which include overawing the witnesses, the turning of the inquiry body into a committee, and an outcome which is the lowest common denominator of all opinions, in which once again some of the real truth may be lost. In my experience, three reasonably intelligent, well-informed and well-chosen persons can usually agree without much difficulty. It has become usual to entrust lawyers or judges with the president's task of moderating the procedures and seeing that justice is done. It is difficult to quarrel with that degree of discrimination simply because lawyers and judges are by long habit steeped in the fundamental requirements of natural justice and of maintaining balance and direction in the inquisitorial process. No one wants an inquiry to be abortive for lack of following the rules of natural justice. Nor has everyone the perception of relevance which judicial proceedings demand if they are ever to come to an end.

Sometimes an inquiry is endowed with powers to compel the attendance of witnesses and the production of documents, as is the case when a statutory inquiry is set up under the *Tribunals and Inquiries Act 1992*. Strangely, the absence of these powers has seldom in my experience caused any problems. Most people involved in a serious matter are willing to give evidence voluntarily. If compelled to attend, they are usually unwilling and unforthcoming witnesses, if not actually unreliable. Moreover those most concerned are either anxious to produce papers supporting their contentions or fearful that if they do not, their refusal will be seen as an admission of guilt and responsibility. As for the swearing-in of witnesses, with which the media have one of their irrational obsessions, this is one of the most fanciful of their many mythologies, such as that which makes them believe that all judges have a mallet with which they regularly bang their desks. Every person who pleads Not Guilty to some charge in a criminal court and is then found guilty by a jury has probably been lying on his oath from beginning to end.

I do not believe that an honest person is more likely to tell the truth merely because he or she has sworn by Almighty God to do so. Nor in my experience is a dishonest person any the less determined to mislead everybody because he lives in fear of divine retribution. Some more familiar with the law than most might have a thought about being charged with perjury, a very rare happening and never much of a deterrent in my time at the Bar.

In any case the truth is a very elusive concept. Many honest people have a perception of some event which is entirely at variance with that of other honest persons, or which can be shown by more powerful evidence to be completely mistaken. Salvador de Madariaga concludes one of his novels with the words: 'What is truth? Truth? The aroma of a bunch of errors.'

5

Some Reflections on Public Inquiries

Louis Blom-Cooper

The public inquiry has become a permanent feature of modern government as an instrument of dampening or dissembling public disquiet about a scandal or a disaster. The fact that since May 1994, when the Department of Health issued its Circular (94)27 requiring health authorities to set up an independent inquiry whenever a mental patient had been involved in a homicide, there has been a number of 'Inquiries after Homicide', is testimony to the spate, not to say plethora of public inquiries, even in the limited field of the mental health system.[1] It is entirely appropriate that anyone engaged in the inquiry process, as we have been, should therefore ask: is the expansive and expensive method of an inquiry justified, in terms of the aims and purposes of good government?

Whenever a scandal or a disaster occurs, arousing public disquiet beyond the immediate scene and attracting national interest and concern, there is a number of reasons why resort should be had to a public inquiry, rather than place reliance upon governmental action or court proceedings, either civil or criminal. The most compelling reason is that the scandalous or disastrous event – particularly where there is a loss of human life – demands the assuaging of public revulsion or repugnance that will not be satisfied by the traditional methods of remedial action. Such public outrage often calls for instantaneous response from government. It may be difficult, if not politically dangerous, to resist the instant demands for an inquiry. The Departmental Circular (94)27 itself is one example of governmental acknowledgement of the social response to violent and unnatural deaths at the hands of mental patients for whose care and treatment health authorities and social services bear responsibility. Such an event understandably demands prompt and adequate means of explaining to an aroused public why and how it happened. Does the public at that stage need to be told who was responsible for it happening? That question goes to the scope of the public inquiry and does not lessen the public's desire to know what happened.

The events which call for independent investigation may often involve allegations of fault by government or other public authorities, or by professionals performing public services. The only viable method of allaying public fears of a cover-up by the organisations involved is to provide for a public inquiry, independent of those with a vested interest in the outcome. Scandals and disasters giving rise to public fears and anxiety about repetition thus extend beyond the interests of individual victims who may have a cause of action for some legal remedy in the courts.

In homicide cases, where there may be little or no dependency and when the bereavement award to a surviving spouse or parents of a child victim under the age of eighteen – currently fixed under the criminal injuries compensation scheme at £10,000 – is inadequate, the victim's entitlement is of central importance (Paul Rock's chapter in this book powerfully makes the case for official recognition of the role of the victim). It is becoming clear that these families are only faintly accommodated within the system of criminal justice. And where the criminal trial is peremptorily disposed of with a plea of guilty and the hospitalisation of the offender, there is less than complete satisfaction in what is publicly revealed in the courtroom. Too much is left unexplained. Since, moreover, the cause of death will have been determined by way of forensic pathology, the role and function of the coroner's inquest will have been fully performed. It cannot strictly go beyond determining how the victim died. A public inquiry provides an opportunity for all those directly affected by the homicide to have their say. (We have been forcibly struck by the dignified manner in which the three children of Mr and Mrs Wilson supported the Inquiry and their ability to observe and speak at the Inquiry.)

It is not just the families of victims of homicide who can

properly demand our attention. The cathartic effect of a public inquiry for the families of homicide victims does not end at the domestic hearth. Often the impact of a homicide disturbs the equilibrium of friends and associates, even a whole community. We have been conscious of how deeply affected the community in the village of Bramford has been. The residents of the Suffolk dormitory to Ipswich too are entitled to expect public recognition of their psychological needs. Individual counselling goes beyond comfort and support for those closest to the victims of homicide. A public inquiry can function by way of pacifying communal feelings. It may just as readily feed a public appetite for the prurient and even accentuate public disquiet about the event.

Finally, a public inquiry, in addition to establishing what happened, may assign responsibility for what happened, although we recognise that the ambit of the inquiry, extending to matters which touch on discipline, may properly rest exclusively with those possessing the power of dismissal from office, or to impose a different sanction. A public inquiry will inevitably, in the unfolding of the events under scrutiny, point to lessons that can be learned. We appreciate that the question whether the public inquiry is the proper place for lesson-learning is a matter for debate, even acute controversy. That feature, however, does not invalidate the need for inquiry. It is relevant to the nature and extent of the role and function of the inquiry. The sponsoring authority, in giving an inquiry precise terms of reference, may properly seek a report which spells out the lessons to be learned.

The report of the Committee of Inquiry into Complaints about Ashworth Hospital recommended that the Government should consider undertaking a thorough review of public inquiries.[2] No public response has been forthcoming from Government. We are aware that the Department of Health is giving urgent consideration to the consequences of the Circular (94)27 of May 1994. That should produce a review of at least 'Inquiries after Homicide'. So far, so good. But we were struck forcibly by a contribution made at the public seminar on 3 November by Professor Olive Stevenson, who wrote an impressive dissenting report in the Maria Colwell Inquiry of 1974. She made the telling point that the opposition to the rash of child abuse inquiries of the late

1980s had sensibly led to the establishment of standing bodies, known as Area Child Protection Committees. While these Committees have worked well, responding instantly to cases of child abuse needing independent investigation, they have increasingly experienced the interplay of social services and mental health services in many of the cases. They have felt ill-equipped to take on the added dimension. Is there not, she asked, a case for an amalgam of the parallel services in the form of joint area committees to cover social services and health authorities – an extension of a multi-disciplinary approach to intertwined social problems?

Inquiry procedures

It is axiomatic that the twin aims of any public inquiry are thoroughness and fairness. The first of these aims is largely self-explanatory. Within terms of reference given to it by the sponsoring authority, the Inquiry must seek to establish the truth of what happened. In this respect it differs markedly from either civil litigation or criminal trial. Central to the adversarial model of civil proceedings between party and party, which demands that the rival disputants direct their cases in their own way, is the fact of parties deciding what evidence is to be adduced to further their respective cases, and the court or tribunal functioning almost exclusively as an impartial umpire, exhibiting an Olympian aloofness from the dust of forensic contest. In the criminal trial the rules of evidence are so restrictive as to make the process only the semblance of truth. Furthermore, the sole purpose of the process is for the prosecution to establish, according to a high standard of proof, its case against the accused; the accused may remain silent, merely putting the adversary to proof. The public inquiry jettisons any such notion of the adversarial paradigm. It seeks a non-adjudicative investigation. There is, however, no other limitation on the search for the truth. No rules of evidence pertain. The only test is whether material is relevant to the task of a thorough investigation. Hence the concept of the inquisitorial nature of public inquiries.

Given that remit, the problem for the inquiring body is how to achieve procedural fairness in the process of decision-making which may involve, directly or indirectly, criticising conduct short of, or encompassing, blameworthiness. The English common lawyer is over-influenced by the adversarial paradigm. The adversarial process for him is culturally conditioned as well as being a legally correct response. He or she instinctively turns to the adversarial model as providing the greatest measure of procedural protection for the client. There lies the rub. In the forensic contest the advocate is the mouthpiece of his client. Apart from certain ethical considerations laid down by the judges and professional bodies, the advocate's duty is first and foremost to represent the client's interests rather than to search for the truth. Notwithstanding this natural and understandable tendency to function in the legal tradition, there is a growing recognition that the adversarial model is inappropriate when applied to the inquisitorial nature of public inquiries, at least in their unreconstructed form. That form is exemplified in notice of complaint (the writ or the indictment); disclosure of documentary material (discovery in civil proceedings); orality of proceedings (criminal trials and most civil actions), confrontation and cross-examination of witnesses; and a reasoned decision (except for juries whose verdicts are definitionally inscrutable) based on the evidence adduced.

Sir Richard Scott, in a lecture entitled, 'Procedures at inquiries – the duty to be fair', clarified the confusing picture portrayed by successive public inquiries.[3] He stated:

> ... the adoption of procedures that translate an inquisitional Inquiry into a series of adversarial issues, with the Inquiry on one side and a shifting collection of individuals on the other side of each issue, is likely, depending on the nature of the Inquiry, to be a grave impediment to the proper functioning of the Inquiry.[4]

Sir Richard went on to conclude that impediment there may have to be, if fairness to individuals against whom criticism is being made cannot otherwise be achieved. But the impediment is avoidable, provided that one's 'vision is not blinkered by an inability to see beyond the procedures of adversarial litigation.'[5] His target was the unreasoning and unreasonable insistence upon a witness who feels in jeopardy of criticism, let alone the pointer of culpability, having his/her lawyer present (if necessary, throughout the Inquiry) to cross-examine his/her critics. In the 'Arms to Iraq' Inquiry, Sir Richard disallowed legal representation in the full-blown sense of asking questions, but administered written questionnaires in advance, whose answers were, or could be drafted by legal advisers. Orality of procedure for eliciting evidence was thus reduced to an irreducible minimum, simply because questioning was self-restricted by the Inquirer and his counsel.

The safeguard for fairness built in to such a process is infected at a late stage of the Inquiry. It is now common practice for passages in the draft of the report, which indicate criticism, to be submitted to the individual for comment and, if necessary, refutation, even with reference to fresh documentation. The process is inevitably lengthy, even inordinately protracted. By contrast, if full legal representation is permissible throughout the Inquiry, no further opportunity to make submissions is, or should be afforded. The Inquiry, like a court or tribunal delivering judgment, proceeds to make its report to the sponsoring authority. Unlike a court delivering its judgment without outside authorisation, there is no power in the Inquiry to initiate publication. That is a matter exclusively for the sponsoring authority to whom it reports. It may publish the report in full or in part. It may or may not expurgate passages it thinks should not be out in the open. It may, of course, decide to give those criticised an opportunity of replying before publication takes place, for the purpose of allowing those individuals a chance to prepare a public statement at the moment of publication. Since the Inquiry cannot effect any disciplinary or other like action against an individual, but can influence only those authorised to take disciplinary action, there is no question, directly, of double jeopardy. The jeopardy lies solely in any adverse verdict of the reporter.

The arguments for or against the one method rather than the other will rumble on. They will no doubt be raised as and when Sir Richard Scott's report is made public – probably contemporaneously with the publication of this book. But Sir Richard's prescription for fairness to individuals deprived of full legal representation has a twist to it which surfaced in October 1995 in the *Review of Prison Security in England and Wales* by General Sir John Learmont KCB, CBE.[6]

Sir John adopted the technique of not allowing witnesses any legal representation, although members of the prison service – prison officers and governors – could have a legal representative or 'friend' present during the witness's interview. There was, however, no confrontation of witnesses. Each was interviewed *seriatim* in private. Unlike the 'Arms to Iraq' Inquiry, public servants were allowed to give their evidence behind closed doors; indeed, they were promised both confidentiality and anonymity. Sir John, in his report states that

> requests have been received for details of evidence and identities of witnesses. These requests have not been met, for to do so would violate the confidentiality and absolute anonymity guaranteed to all.[7]

He adds, to justify the exceptional immunity, that

> the Inquiry has collected a considerable amount of evidence from people at all levels within the [Prison] Service who would feel extremely vulnerable if the pledge which has been given was not honoured.

Just so. But why was the pledge given in the first place? May not the Director of the Prison Service, who, in the light of Sir John's Report, was dismissed by the Secretary of State for the Home Department, have a legitimate grievance that he had no opportunity of testing or answering the criticisms made of him by who knows whom?

The art of conducting public inquiries is in a state of flux. There is a pressing need for official guidance. A review of Circular (94)27 of May 1994 on 'Inquiries after Homicide' provides a golden opportunity to show the way forward.

Notes

1. See Appendix B.
2. *Report of the Committee of Inquiry into Complaints about Ashworth Hospital* (1992) Cm 2028-I, at 35.
3. Delivered to the Chancery Bar Association on 2 May 1995 and

reproduced as (1995) 'Procedures at inquiries – the duty to be fair', *Law Quarterly Review* III, 596-616.

4. Ibid., at 611.

5. Ibid., at 611.

6. *Review of Prison Security in England and Wales* (1995) Cm 3020.

7. Ibid., at para 1.25.

6

Psychiatric Inquiries:
Learning the Lessons

John Crichton and David Sheppard

Psychiatric inquiries may have a long heritage but never have they been so numerous or so costly. In Britain, from the late 1960s to the mid 1980s, there were regular psychiatric public inquiries, mostly focusing on abuses and over-restrictive practices within institutions.[1] Recent inquiries into psychiatric care mark a shift in British public opinion: away from concern about the abuse of power within institutions, towards anxiety about the lack of control in the community.[2] 1995 has seen an explosion in the number of psychiatric inquiries, all focused on homicides committed by the mentally disordered.[3] This chapter discusses some of the problems with this inquiry industry and concludes that the present situation cannot continue. Moreover, the chapter identifies, among others, one particularly important role of inquiries, that of audit: of learning the lessons. Currently there is a risk that important lessons will not be learnt because of a number of factors which will be discussed, not least 'inquiry fatigue'. Finally there are some suggestions about how the goal of disseminating the important lessons from these tragic events may be better achieved.

Background

Yesterday's 'scandals' of the Institution have already been replaced by today's 'scandals' of the community.[4]

1992 saw the death of Jonathan Zito, killed by Christopher

Clunis; the visit of Ben Silcock to the lions' den at London Zoo; and the killing of Katy Sullivan, a worker at a London MIND hostel, by a patient.[5] Nicholas Rose's observation in 1986, quoted above, seemed to be confirmed. The Royal College of Psychiatrists (RCP) had for some time petitioned for greater powers of control in the community, but these proposals had lost steam in the late 1980s when the suggestions for compulsory treatment in the community were roundly condemned by both government and user groups. At the end of 1992 new proposals had been formulated. The RCP's 'Community Supervision Order' proposals would allow the compulsory admission for treatment of a patient known to relapse when not taking medication, at the point of non-compliance rather than the point of relapse.[6] The government's response not only to the College, but to scandals in the community, rising public concern and pressure from user and relatives' groups, such as NSF and SANE, was to set up an internal review of the legal powers over the mentally ill in the community.[7] In August 1993 the report was published, together with Virginia Bottomley's 'Ten Point Plan'.[8] This plan of action led to a number of government initiatives:

- The *Mental Health (Patients in the Community) Act 1995*, due to come into force early in 1996,[9] which is based on the Department of Health's internal review and is essentially a revision of, although not a replacement for, existing guardianship powers.[10] Controversially, it would allow the key worker of a patient on an order the power of arrest should the patient fail to comply with the order, so that an examination for compulsory hospital admission under existing admission criteria could be carried out.
- Supervision registers: psychiatric services were obliged to set up a register of patients thought to be at particular risk of violence to others, suicide or self-neglect.[11] The creation of such a register was proposed by the Clunis Inquiry and was intended to help direct care to the most vulnerable patients and prevent them from 'slipping through the net' of psychiatric care;[12] as such it might better be described as a 'prioritisation register'. However, it was seen by many clinicians as a measure simply to pacify public anxiety; it

implied that psychiatrists had supervisory powers over registered patients in the community and would therefore be held responsible for the actions of those patients.[13]

- Guidance on Risk Assessment and Discharge.[14] Largely welcomed by psychiatric professionals, this briefing document gives advice on risk assessment and management. This less publicized measure was perhaps initially somewhat eclipsed by its more controversial bed-fellows. However, the guidance also contained the instruction that when psychiatric patients under follow-up committed homicide an independent inquiry should be held, although an internal inquiry was suggested as being adequate in response to a suicide. It was perhaps not the intention that this advice would fuel a booming inquiry industry. It can be estimated that psychiatric patients under follow-up may commit between ten to thirty homicides a year,[15] a rate which has not increased over recent years.[16] Combined with a rough estimate that some recent public inquiries have cost £250,000 each, the cost to the health service per annum of such inquiries is estimated at several million pounds per year. Also, as the number of learned reports mount up, their impact on clinical practice outside those immediately involved becomes limited. The psychiatric professions risk becoming dismissive of this irritating rash of reports and not heeding the important lessons that these tragic cases illustrate.

The original guidance on the conduct of homicide inquiries was subject to minor revision by the Department of Health in November 1995 in their *Building Bridges* guide.[17] This document also contains a paragraph about the costs of an inquiry and the importance of getting value for money.

The aims of inquiries

Elsewhere in this book other contributors have commented on the diverse and possibly conflicting aims behind inquiries. Nowhere is this more apparent than in the recent 'Inquiries after Homicide'. It is certainly an aim of central government to show that problems with community care are being addressed comprehensively and robustly, albeit at a local level, so that public confidence can be restored. Another aim may be to find out if an individual was to blame for a particular tragic event, to point the finger and to identify those responsible for a tragedy.

Then there are the concerns of victims' families, who quite rightly are often involved in the inquiry process. They themselves, however, may still be in the throes of grieving and have mixed feelings about what aims the inquiry should have. In our experience of talking to many victims' families, their principal concern is not primarily retribution or compensation, but a desire that lessons should be learnt from tragic events, so that similar tragedies may better be avoided; and so that loved ones will not have died in vain. For an example, consider the tone, as well as the content, of this letter, published in the *Psychiatric Bulletin*:

Dear Sir

I am a parent whose mentally disordered son died partly because of a lack of community care. Grieving parents and loved ones need to know that lessons from the past are learnt, so that future tragedies might be best avoided. This I have found frustrating. I would like to share with your readers some ideas about future research.

Sometimes mentally disordered people are refused admission to a psychiatric unit or abruptly discharged because of a violent act or the suggestion of a history of violence. This certainly seemed to happen in the case of Christopher Clunis; the more disturbed he became the less effective his care became. Surely there should be research about how many patients are refused admission or abruptly discharged and what subsequently happens to them.

There seem to be problems about confidentiality when carers contact psychiatric services with their concerns over patients who are becoming violent or aggressive. There is a need for guidelines about how such calls from carers are handled by psychiatric units and those guidelines should be subject to clinical audit. Sometimes it feels like concerned carers are simply ignored and no action seems to be taken.

There seems to be hardly any research about the safety of carers. Life threatening assault may be rare but frightening assaults and aggressive behaviour are very common. It can disrupt family life leading to young family members staying away because of safety fears and chronic disruption of carers' sleep.

There seems to be a real problem with police liaison and patients sometimes fall between the police and the psychiatric services neither willing to step in. There needs to be guidelines about what information is passed on to the police. I hope your readers find these thoughts of some help as they continue to try and make community care work; if it is to work carers need to be listened to.

Yours faithfully, Michelle Twigg[18]

There are other mechanisms to decide criminal responsibility, civil claims of negligence, or breaches of professional conduct, but it is only in the context of a public inquiry that a thorough and open review may be (and may be seen to be) accomplished with recommendations publicised nationwide. Indeed, the importance of audit in response to the whole range of untoward incidents which may occur is stressed in recent official guidance:

> Even in the best run service the possibility remains that something may go wrong. It is essential that all those in planning, purchasing and providing mental health services are seen to investigate any serious incident involving a mentally ill person quickly and objectively, and to learn lessons from any inquiry.[19]

The widow of Jonathan Zito, Jayne, has turned her energies to the formation of the Zito Trust which sponsored a review of recent inquiries and highlighted their conclusions.[20] Whereas local services were seen to heed the advice of a local inquiry, there was the impression that the dissemination of important lessons to a wider audience had not taken place and that professionals were not appraising themselves of inquiry recommendations, even when they were well distributed.

Part of the problem may simply be the mass of information produced with several recent inquiries running to hundreds of pages. The inquiry reports vary greatly in style and layout and each one needs to be approached differently to uncover its key points. Whereas in past years it could be said that mental health professionals should at least be aware of the key recommendations of major inquiries, now it requires much more effort. If page length is used as a guide, at least five times the amount of material is required to be read in 1995 compared to 1994. If the

list of pending inquiries found in Appendix B can be used as a guide, there may be another five-fold increase in 1996. This is undoubtedly a problem if the main lessons from psychiatric inquiries are to be digested.

There is also a problem about the availability of inquiry reports. There is no central repository of reports: neither the Mental Health Act Commission, nor the Royal College of Psychiatrists, nor MIND, nor the copyright library at Cambridge University, has a complete series. Sometimes this is because the reports are published in-house, not formally copyrighted, and are available only on request. There have been occasions on which the print run has been so small – for example, the Blackwood Inquiry[21] – that interested professionals have been unable to obtain a copy. Sometimes summaries of inquiries are published in professional journals, but no journal has a policy of commissioning papers on all inquiries and expediting their publication while the issues are still fresh and immediately relevant.

Sensitivity to inquiries

Many professionals may only learn about the latest inquiry via the media. Newspaper articles may not, however, focus on the most clinically relevant material and may not accurately report an inquiry's findings. In the case of the Robinson Inquiry, most media attention focused on suggestions for law reform and critical comments about current government policy.[22] Within the report these comments made up only a small part of the conclusions; the clinically relevant lessons about risk assessment and discharge were not discussed by the media in any detail. The Robinson Inquiry could be criticised for straying too widely from the focus of the case in its discussion of law reform,[23] while the whole topic of the role and form of such inquiries is beginning to attract debate.[24]

There is perhaps a feeling within the professions that such inquiries will be unreasonably critical, not only of professional groups but of named individuals. There can be little doubt that to come under the scrutiny of a public inquiry is profoundly stressful and there almost appears to be hostility to such scrutiny among the psychiatric professions. If an inquiry merely engenders defensive hostility and thereby cannot achieve open and frank examination of a tragedy, then it has failed. If an inquiry leaves a hospital or community service crushed and demoralised, with no corporate hope or vision, then, unless it recommends the complete replacement of that service, it has also failed. If an inquiry can gain the trust of those placed under examination and if it can be truly constructive in its criticisms, then not only will the service concerned respond more favourably to the findings, but the professions as a whole are more likely to receive recommendations favourably.

A major concern is the exposure of individual mental health workers to unreasonable scrutiny, either in the public hearings, often reported or occasionally televised extensively in the local media, or in the inquiry reports. Most recent inquiries have found multiple failures in the systems of current care, rather than in individuals. In cases where it is apparent that a system rather than an individual is under scrutiny, staff could be reassured that their personal blame was not of principal concern, rather that it was their role in the system which could be improved. Elsewhere in this book it is suggested that disciplinary proceedings separate and prior to the public inquiry may help reduce the immense pressure put on staff.

At times the collection of inquiry reports feels more akin to stamp collecting than clinical psychiatry. Sometimes the tracking down of a scarce report and examination of an inquiry's method can obscure the importance of its contents. If the current rash of inquiry reports are not widely read and do not influence practice then they risk being as nationally relevant as a private stamp collection. Worse still, they might have a clearly negative, antagonistic effect. Inquiry reports will always contain minor errors, will always miss important details, will almost always contain recommendations which are controversial, but if they are dismissed before they are read and fail to engender a debate of the issues, then a valuable opportunity for improving national practice will be lost.

Ten suggestions for reform of 'Inquiries after Homicide'

(1) Clarification of purpose

The aim of recent inquiries has not always been clear and the terms under which they are established can be very vague. Even the official guidance into homicide inquiries leaves a large amount of scope for interpretation.[25] We would agree with official policy that a principal aim should be that of clinical audit, where systems rather than individuals are under examination and the lessons learnt are aimed at national distribution. There may be a need for more comprehensive guidance for those who commission inquiries and those asked to conduct them.

(2) Ensuring the independence and expertise of inquiry members

There is currently need for guidance to help the selection of those who should make up an inquiry team and decide whether or not they are aided by legal counsel. Inquiry members should be of sufficient stature and reputation; yet, together with the advantages that brings, there is a risk that well-known figures may use inquiries as vehicles for promulgating views that they hold dear. As Chiswick comments, if inquiry members are to adopt the role of investigative journalists, they must not make the error of making themselves out to be more important than the story.[26] There is a danger that homicide cases are used to inform policy which will affect the vast majority of patients who have not been, and are never likely to be, associated with such tragedy, and that incorporated into inquiry reports are ideas for national policy only tenuously related to the case at hand.

(3) Increased sensitivity to the needs of victims and / or their families

There may be many victims, some not so obvious, associated with psychiatric homicide inquiries. By bitter irony both the victim's and perpetrator's families in the Robinson Inquiry shared the same surname, helping to illustrate that they were both, in different ways, victims. In that Inquiry there can also be identified a number of individuals who could be called victims: those who had been subject to previous assault, those subject to malicious correspondence, professionals who had been let down by their managers, resource restraints or the law. In the case of homicide the victim's family should be the focus of particular support. They may require legal or medical advice, they will certainly require the name of an individual who can liaise between them and the inquiry team and they may well require use of a room, away from the eyes of the media, during public hearings.

(4) Establishing an accessible and readable style

Many people picking up an inquiry report will have little time to read through it in detail, they will want to see a clear summary and set of recommendations. Inquiry reports were once written in 'turgid civil servese: nobody read them apart from the proof reader';[27] on the other hand an overly literary or dramatic style has been criticised.[28]

(5) Producing a summary of the key issues

Following from the previous point, a summary of the key issues could be prepared and, for example, distributed to all the employees of hospitals which had been involved in the case. A brief summary should include the reason for the inquiry taking place, the terms of reference, conclusions and recommendations.

(6) Clear identification of issues of national importance

Some recommendations will clearly be local in their focus, but the reader's eye should be drawn to those recommendations which have national significance and relevance.

(7) Linking issues in the report to earlier inquiries and research

As a body of knowledge is established, recommendations which have been made in previous inquiries may be echoed. Greater weight may be put upon a recommendation if several inquiries have come to similar conclusions. A useful chapter in any inquiry report would be one which comments on any similarities to previous investigations. Some inquiries have included academic seminar days, such as the one from which this publication has arisen. Such an approach helps a deeper examination of the issues raised and fosters a healthy sense of self-examination. However, the benefits must be weighed against the additional costs involved.

(8) Distributing the report widely

There should be a list of key organisations and journals to which inquiry reports should be automatically distributed. It is greatly confusing when some reports can be found in bookshops while others are only available upon written request, and it is often unclear to whom to write.

(9) Follow-up by the inquiry team

It should be part of any inquiry that the team is reassembled to comment upon the implementation of their recommendations locally. Following the Ashworth Inquiry the Health Advisory Service were approached to comment on the progress of the hospital and addressed all ninety of the original inquiry's recommendations;[29] yet following the Blackwood Inquiry a public request from the team to return and review improvements was refused.[30] The Newby Inquiry team were asked to perform a follow-up report only after a public request by Jayne Zito at the Inquiry's launch.[31] At some point following the submission of an inquiry report, those who sponsored the report should make a formal response, detailing what action they plan to make in the light of the recommendations.

(10) National audit of the inquiry recommendations

There needs to be some mechanism which ensures that recommendations are considered for incorporation into national policy, publicised and subsequently audited. The first stage of clinical audit involves the identification of a problem; this is akin to an inquiry's investigation of the facts of a case. The next stage is setting a standard: an inquiry may recommend a standard, but currently there is no mechanism whereby an inquiry's recommendations are systematically considered by policy makers and professional organisations. There then should follow a comparison of agreed standards and actual practice. However, this last stage cannot be achieved without some pre-existing mechanism to agree upon those standards.

Conclusions

The current practices surrounding psychiatric inquiries are bound to fail: recent inquiries have, at times, lacked sufficient clarity in their purpose and scope; they cost too much; services under the spotlight are put under huge and perhaps unreasonable strain; the number and length of inquiry reports is overwhelming; and the important lessons which need to be learnt are being obscured by peripheral issues and are not communicated to those who would benefit from them. There is, therefore, the need for further revision of the guidance on when a public inquiry is to be called, what form it should take, how it should be published and publicised, and what local follow-up arrangements should be in place.

It may be valuable to consider whether there should be a central clearing house for inquiries, linking together incidents with similar themes for investigation, responsible for appointing inquiry members and standardising the publication of reports. One candidate for that role would be the Mental Health Act Commission, but that would involve a change of its role and remit. The summaries from inquiries and comment about any trends they reveal could then be incorporated into the Commission's published reports. Such an approach would help the process of digesting the lessons from inquiries and arriving at nationally agreed standards which could then be audited. Costs could also be reduced by establishing an experienced secretariat to support inquiries, and by avoiding one possible reason for escalating costs: that those commissioning inquiries are unlikely to wish to invite the criticism that they have spent less then other similar inquiries.

Society needs to accept that if community psychiatric care is to be adopted then psychiatric services cannot contain or minimise risk in the same way as when most psychiatric patients were behind the high-walled, isolated asylums. The psychiatric professions need to accept that community care involves a widening of their accountability and of the scrutiny that they will undergo following tragedy. The control over patients in the community must balance legitimate public concerns and individual respect for patients and their rights. There are dangers at both extremes represented by the two types of inquiry found in recent years; neither over-control and abuse within institutions nor under-control and lack of supervision is acceptable. But striking a reasonable balance of control in the community is fraught with problems and in perpetual danger of satisfying neither the side which campaigns for widespread reinstitutionalisation nor those who champion patients' rights.

Acknowledgement

Parts of this paper were published in J.H.M. Crichton (1996) 'The Falling Shadow: comment on the Robinson Inquiry', *Psychiatric Care* 3, no 1.

Notes

1. Martin J. (1984) *Hospitals in Trouble*, Oxford, Basil Blackwell.
2. Crichton J.H.M. (1995) 'The response to psychiatric inpatient violence', in J.H.M. Crichton (ed.) *Psychiatric Patient Violence: Risk and Response*, London, Duckworth.
3. See Appendix B.
4. Rose N. (1986) 'Law, rights and psychiatry', in P. Miller and N. Rose (eds) *The Power of Psychiatry*, Cambridge, Polity Press, at 206.
5. See Ritchie J.H. (Chairman) Dick D. & Lingham R. (1994) *The Report of the Inquiry into the Care and Treatment of Christopher Clunis*, London, HMSO; and Utting W. (Chairman) (1994) *Creating*

Community Care. Report of the Mental Health Foundation Inquiry into Community Care for People with Severe Mental Illness, London, The Mental Health Foundation.

6. Royal College of Psychiatrists (1993) *Community Supervision Orders*, London, Royal College of Psychiatrists.

7. DOH (1993a) *Legal Powers on the Care of Mentally Ill People in the Community, Report of the Internal Review*, London, Department of Health.

8. DOH (1993b) Press Release H93/908, 12 August 1993.

9. See Crichton J.H.M. (1994a) 'Supervised Discharge', *Medicine, Science and the Law* 34, 319-20; and Eastman N. (1995) 'Anti-therapeutic community mental health law', *British Medical Journal* 310, 1081-2.

10. DOH (1993a) op. cit.

11. NHS Executive (1994) Introduction of Supervision Registers for Mentally Ill People from 1 April 1994, HSG(94)5, London, Department of Health. See also Harrison G. & Barlett P. (1994) 'Supervision registers for mentally ill people', *British Medical Journal* 309, 551-2; and Royal College of Psychiatrists (1994) 'Supervision registers: the college's response', *Psychiatric Bulletin* 18, 385-6.

12. Ritchie *et al.* (1994) op. cit.

13. Prins H. (1995) 'I've got a little list. But is it any use?', *Medicine, Science and the Law* 35, 218-24.

14. See paras 27 and 28 of NHS Executive (1994) Guidance on the discharge of mentally disordered people and their continuing care in the community, HSG (94)27, London, Department of Health.

15. Boyd W.D. (Director) (1994) *A Preliminary Report on Homicide*, London, The steering committee of the Confidential Inquiry into Homicides and Suicides by Mentally Ill People.

16. Sayce L. (1995) 'Response to violence: a framework for fair treatment' in J.H.M. Crichton (ed.) *Psychiatric Patient Violence: Risk and Response*, London, Duckworth.

17. See paras 5.1.18-21 of DOH (1995) *Building Bridges. A guide to arrangements for inter-agency working for the care and protection of severely mentally ill people*, London, Department of Health. The other revisions are minor and largely matters of emphasis. For example, para 5.1.19.ii no longer mentions considering appointing 'a lawyer as chairman' but merely 'an independent person'; para 5.1.19.iii, relating to the distribution of the inquiry report, now notes that 'An undertaking, given at the start of the process, to publish the report enhances the credibility of the inquiry'.

18. Twigg M. (1994) 'Making community care work', *Psychiatric Bulletin* 18, 701-2.

19. DOH (1995) op. cit., at para 5.1.1.

20. Sheppard D. (1995) *Learning the Lessons. Mental Health Inquiry reports published in England and Wales between 1969-1994 and their* *recommendations for improving practice*, London, Zito Trust (copies available from Zito Trust, PO Box 265 London, WC2H 9JD).

21. See Prins H. (Chairman) (1993) *Report of the Committee of Inquiry into the death at Broadmoor Hospital of Orville Blackwood and a review of the deaths of two other Afro-Caribbean patients: 'Big, black and dangerous?'* London, Special Hospitals Service Authority; and Crichton J.H.M. (1994b) 'Comment on the Blackwood Inquiry', *Psychiatric Bulletin* 18, 236-7.

22. The Robinson Inquiry appears as Blom-Cooper L., Halley H. & Murphy E. (1995) *The Falling Shadow: one patient's mental health care 1978-1993*, London, Duckworth.

23. See Bynoe I. (1995) 'The Falling Shadow: a lawyer's view', *Journal of Forensic Psychiatry* 6, 588-93; and Chiswick D. (1995) 'The Falling Shadow: a psychiatrist's view', *Journal of Forensic Psychiatry* 6, 594-600.

24. Bowden P. (1995) 'Confidential inquiry into homicides and suicides by mentally ill people. A preliminary report on homicide', *Psychiatric Bulletin* 19, 65-6.

25. See Appendix A.

26. Chiswick (1995) op. cit.

27. Ibid.

28. Bynoe (1995) op. cit.; Chiswick (1995) op. cit.

29. See Blom-Cooper L. (Chairman) (1992) *Report of the Committee of Inquiry into Complaints about Ashworth Hospital*, Cm 2028-I, London, HMSO; and the response by the Health Advisory Service (1995) *With Care in Mind Secure: A review for the Special Hospitals Service Authority of the services provided by Ashworth Hospital*, Sutton, National Health Service Health Advisory Services.

30. Prins (1993) op. cit.

31. Davies N. (Chairman), Lingham R., Prior C. & Sims A. (1995) *Report of the Inquiry into the circumstances leading to the death of Jonathan Newby (a volunteer worker) on 9th October 1993 in Oxford*, Oxford, Oxford Health Authority.

Reflections on Child Abuse Inquiries[1]

Peter Reder and Sylvia Duncan

It is believed that between one and three children a week in England and Wales die from abuse inflicted by their parents.[2] Over the years, an extensive network of professionals has collaborated to protect children from maltreatment, including social workers, the NSPCC, health visitors, doctors, psychologists, the police, judges, teachers and nurses. The key practitioners are social workers, who have responsibility for investigating concerns about children's safety and for protecting them from harm. The other professionals are required to work together with social services and with each other in order to give priority to children's needs.[3] Area Child Protection Committees (ACPCs) help co-ordinate the work of different agencies, produce inter-agency guidelines of appropriate procedures in suspected child abuse cases and hold Child Protection Registers of the names of children for whom a protection plan is deemed necessary.

The functioning of child protection networks has become progressively more sophisticated as a result of research, experience, training and supervision, but a particular influence has been the long history of high-profile inquiries into the deaths of children known to statutory agencies. After an inquiry into the death while in foster care of Denis O'Neill,[4] there appears to have been an interval until the early 1970s when the cases of Graham Bagnall and then Maria Colwell hit the headlines.[5] Since then, there has been an average of two major public inquiries a year into child abuse tragedies,[6] recently accompanied by a series of investigations into groups of child sexual abuse cases.[7]

The conclusions of these inquiries have undoubtedly made a

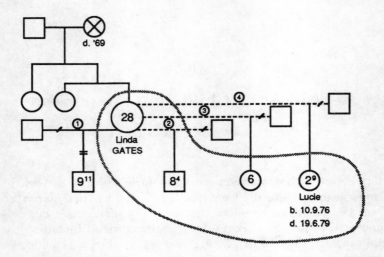

Figure 1. Genogram of Lucie Gates' family as it was at the time of her death (reproduced from Reder, Duncan and Gray, *Beyond Blame*, Routledge, 1993, with the publisher's permission). See p. 82 below.

difference to professional practice and to wider social policy, but their process has given rise to so much disquiet that many have questioned their value. In this chapter, we shall first outline work that we have been engaged on to reconsider cases at the centre of fatal child abuse inquiries in order to draw additional lessons from them. Then, we shall reflect on the costs and benefits of the inquiries to date and offer a view on what has limited the learning derived from them. Finally, we wish to suggest a process that could overcome these problems.

Beyond Blame

In 1985, we were members of a child mental health team which based its work on the family systems approach, with its emphasis on understanding inter-personal relationships and the wider context of behaviour. We had a particular interest in applying these ideas to problems of child abuse and the functioning of multi-agency professional networks and decided to review all

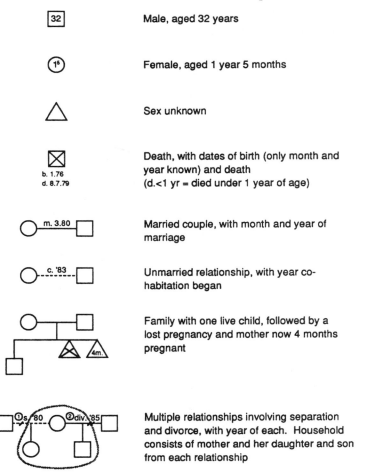

32	Male, aged 32 years
1⁵	Female, aged 1 year 5 months
△	Sex unknown
⊠ b. 1.76 d. 8.7.79	Death, with dates of birth (only month and year known) and death (d.<1 yr = died under 1 year of age)
○ m. 3.80 □	Married couple, with month and year of marriage
○ c. '83 □	Unmarried relationship, with year co-habitation began
	Family with one live child, followed by a lost pregnancy and mother now 4 months pregnant
	Multiple relationships involving separation and divorce, with year of each. Household consists of mother and her daughter and son from each relationship

Figure 2. Common genogram symbols (adapted from Reder, Duncan and Gray, *Beyond Blame*, Routledge, 1993, with the publisher's permission) See p. 82 below.

available inquiry reports into fatal child abuse to see whether our clinical approach could help us re-analyse the cases at the centre of the inquiries and allow new lessons to emerge.

With some difficulty, we managed to obtain 35 reports, published in the United Kingdom between 1973 and 1989, and reviewed each case by first drawing the family's genogram, or family tree (see figures 1 and 2 on pp. 80-1 for an example)[8] and writing out in sequence the chronology of events. We particularly highlighted transitions in the family (such as births and losses), problems shown by the family, professional responses and the effects of these interventions. Then we went through the case in detail, pausing regularly to generate hypotheses about what had happened, in the same way that we would in a complex case referred to the clinical team. After that, we compared our ideas about all the cases to identify patterns common to them. We organised the patterns into three main themes: relationships within the families, interactions among members of the professional networks and relationships between the families and professionals.

We were able to identify many significant themes, such as: parents usually closed off from contact with professionals during episodes of escalating abuse to their child; some parents gave disguised warnings to professionals that their child was in immediate danger; and some of the children appeared to carry a psychological meaning to their parents that rendered them particularly vulnerable to abuse. Our study and ideas were published in a series of articles[9] and a book entitled *Beyond Blame*.[10] The title was chosen because we became convinced that the preoccupation of many inquiry panels with apportioning blame to professionals for failing to prevent a child's death had limited the lessons that could be learned and, while professionals must be seen to be accountable for their actions, understanding complex cases requires an approach that goes beyond blaming.

Since then, we have presented and discussed our ideas at many conferences around the country and have embarked on an analysis of more cases that have been the subject of local 'Section 8' reviews. We have also consulted to a number of individuals or staff groups that have been involved in cases of serious harm to a child. These experiences have allowed us to reflect on the value of inquiries and their impact on professionals and the practice of child protection.

Benefits, limitations and costs of fatal child abuse inquiries

Benefits

Inquiries into fatal child abuse have been able to influence social policy, sometimes prompting changes in child care legislation, and professional practice in individual cases. As a social phenomenon, they have added to the debate about the relationship between citizens and the state and the role of professionals in the lives of families.[11]

Adcock and Hill have separately discussed some of the wider social and legislative changes that have been the consequence of inquiries.[12] The Denis O'Neill inquiry in 1945 led to the establishment of unified local authority Children's Departments responsible for children unable to live with their natural families. The Children Act that followed in 1948 emphasised keeping families together and encouraged local authorities to rehabilitate children with their family of origin. The inquiry into the death of Maria Colwell a year after she was returned to live with her mother and step-father from a foster family where she had thrived had a profound impact on child care practice.[13] In particular, a belief in the importance of the 'blood tie' was re-evaluated, a policy of permanency in placing children was introduced, the use of at risk registers (now called child protection registers), inter-agency committees and case conferences was advanced and the powers of local authorities relative to parents were substantially strengthened in the *Children Act 1975*. The Kimberley Carlile report highlighted how complex child care law had become and this fed into the revisions already being prepared for the *Children Act 1989*.[14]

In addition, inquiries have brought the issue of child mal-treatment to the attention of the public and raised its profile among practitioners, academics and policy makers. There has been a much greater sensitivity to the problem generally, interest in studying and researching it, developing methods of intervention and drafting legislation and guidelines which prioritise children's needs. The balance of work undertaken by professionals, most notably social workers, has certainly changed and child protection has now assumed priority within social services departments, with some resources shifted towards that work and posts created to facilitate training and co-ordination. Without doubt, over the last twenty years the literature on child abuse has expanded to a greater extent than probably any other realm of social or psychological interest.

It is more difficult to assess the effects of inquiries on the day-to-day practice of child protection. Inquiry recommendations are frequently disseminated through Department of Health circulars or policy guidance that filter down over subsequent years, and it is left to individual agencies to determine how they translate guidance into practice, leading to local variation. Hallett and Birchall[15] observe that the Department has shown an increased interest in the skill and practice content of social work in abuse cases since the Jasmine Beckford report[16] and has, to some extent, shifted its attention from procedural advice.

One impact of the Maria Colwell case may well be reflected in the following figures: by 1976, two years after publication of the inquiry report, the number of Place of Safety Orders taken out had nearly quadrupled over the number taken out during 1972.[17] During the 1980s, the number of child protection registrations recorded by the NSPCC progressively rose, but the steepest rises were between 1984-6 and 1988-9.[18] The cases which attracted intense media attention during those years were Jasmine Beckford (died July 1984), Tyra Henry (died September 1984) and Kimberley Carlile (died June 1986).[19] Whether these increases reflect greater sensitivity, more appropriate decision taking, or defensive practice is uncertain. However, the NSPCC figures for numbers of registrations of seriously or fatally injured children show a quite dramatic fall immediately after publication of the Maria Colwell inquiry report in 1974.[20]

Limitations

While there have clearly been some benefits as a direct or indirect consequence of child abuse inquiries, their limitations are equally apparent. In a considered critique of their value,

Hallett acknowledges that inquiries have played an important part in shaping local policy, procedures and practice and have offered learnable lessons about recording and transmission of information, assessment, supervision and professional training.[21] However, she doubts whether those lessons have been learned and regrets the lack of government support for improvements in social work training urged in the Jasmine Beckford and Kimberley Carlile reports. Indeed, the Kimberley Carlile panel recommended that the key social workers written submission to the panel should be circulated and used as a training document because it contained such valuable insights into the social worker's role in child protection. We have been told that this never happened and this does not entirely surprise us, since the report also spoke of this same social worker as the 'prime candidate for blameworthiness' and, even though he had gained such an understanding of child protection work, recommended that he should no longer carry any statutory child protection responsibilities!

Dingwall concludes that, because findings of successive reports have a great deal in common, they are failing to make any lasting impact on everyday practice.[22] He believes that this stems from fundamental limitations in the legal approach to the problems involved. Hallett also believes that the lawyers who have chaired so many of the panels have brought particular skills of reconstructing stories in terms of individual actions, but this preoccupation has unfortunately precluded complex events being understood within their context and in relation to other people.[23]

We would concur with these sentiments and cannot accept that the thesis-antithesis-synthesis model upon which legal 'truth' is based is translatable to understanding the nuances of inter-personal behaviour (as is argued in the introduction to the Kimberley Carlile report). The adversarial nature of the Lucie Gates proceedings not only created splits among the inquiry panel itself – two separate reports were produced – but prevented some of them from asking the questions that they felt were relevant.[24] The Tyra Henry panel reflected that: 'much of the questioning of the witnesses, while no doubt helpful to the participants, was not particularly helpful to us.'[25]

Our own re-analysis of cases confirmed that many lessons that could have been learned about inter-personal behaviour have remained latent.[26] For instance, half of the 35 reports we read repeated previous concerns about communication failures among involved professionals. They made useful recommendations about the *structures* necessary for good communication and the *mechanics* of information transfer but failed to address the *psychology* of communication, in which the meaning attributed to messages becomes coloured by non-verbal accompaniments, anxiety, group phenomena, preconceptions, and so on. Such subtleties can never be examined in adversarial settings, where their importance will remain unrecognised.

Costs

It is said that the Jasmine Beckford and Tyra Henry inquiries each cost £250,000 and the Kimberley Carlile inquiry £500,000.[27] But the costs of inquiries go way beyond the financial. At a general level, they pander to everyone's idealised wish that child abuse deaths are 'predictable and preventable' (as the report says of Jasmine Beckford's death) and perhaps even that child abuse itself can be eradicated. The sad reality is that children will continue to be maltreated and killed by their parents and that our ability to predict is limited.[28]

Whether inquiry panels have intended it or not, some employers have used criticisms of individual staff to discipline or dismiss them. One consequence is that some practitioners involved in recent cases (e.g. Tyra Henry and Kimberley Carlile) have declined to participate in the inquiries, presumably because they have lost confidence in them as constructive exercises. The seriousness of this commentary on the whole process should not be underestimated.

Another repercussion is the defensive practice commented upon by Hutchinson, among others, in which decisions are made more for the need to 'cover our backs' and less for the needs of the case.[29] This particularly shows in a slavish adherence to 'the procedures', which precludes any thinking about the case itself. During our reading of the reports for *Beyond Blame* and our current work with Section 8 reviews, we have been struck by the number of panels which focussed on whether the procedures were followed and, if so, concluded that there was little else to learn.[30] Perhaps this represents a defensive approach to the inquiry, but it cannot encourage practitioners to reflect on their work and refine their practice.

The emotional repercussions of inquiries on agencies and practitioners are profound and long lasting. Many have reported that the accompanying media attention, compulsion to find someone to blame and trial-like proceedings make them feel helplessly victimised and powerless to present information that they feel is important.[31] Shearer and Hutchinson have both commented on the devastating effect on a social worker's confidence and morale, which in turn sends waves of unease through the profession and which persists for years afterwards.[32]

We can confirm this from our own experience of presenting *Beyond Blame* around the country. Many professionals have approached us to say that they were involved directly or indirectly with an inquiry and have conveyed how vivid those memories remain. In Brighton, over twenty years after Maria Colwell's death, we were warned to be sensitive to the fact that some practitioners were still involved with members of the Colwell/Kepple family. Most welcomed our attempt to get beyond the blaming attitude that they had experienced. We have become convinced as a result of our consultation work with staff following a child's death or severe injuries that the emotional impact of such events on the professionals is devastating. They are consumed with compassion for the child and with enormous guilt for not having rescued him or her. Even if it is obvious that they could have done nothing to prevent the abuse, their sense of responsibility remains and ripples throughout their agency. This impact is rarely dealt with and instead is compounded by any inquiry process. We shall return to this issue when we propose a different way of responding to the death of a child.

Overall, then, inquiries have made a constructive impact on child protection work but their benefit has been limited and, to many observers, has been outweighed by their social, professional and personal cost.

Inquiries and their conflicting agendas

Many reports demonstrate that the panels thought carefully about the purpose of their inquiries and therefore how they should be conducted. They were usually given a very general remit, as exemplified by the terms of reference quoted in the Tyra Henry report:

> To inquire in public into all the circumstances surrounding the death of Tyra Henry and their relationship to the work of the agencies concerned with her welfare; to draw both particular and general conclusions, and to report.[33]

Some have chosen to widen their brief in order to make recommendations about social policy and legislation. It is unusual for disciplinary matters to be as evident as they were in the agenda for the Jasmine Beckford inquiry, which included: 'to advise what action relating to staffing issues should be taken.' It is much more common to read disclaimers by the panels that the inquiry was not a trial and they were not seeking to allocate blame.

However, the more reports we read, the more it is apparent that they are set up to serve diverse purposes, primarily discipline, learning, catharsis and reassurance. Each agenda is legitimate in its own right but one inquiry cannot satisfy all the different pressures and interests. In our view, it has been the incompatibility, and often the ambiguity, of these different interests that has generated so much concern about the inquiries and limited their benefits.

Discipline

Every professional must be seen to be accountable for his or her actions. If a child known to public agencies dies from maltreatment, it is possible that involved staff made errors of omission or commission, or errors of judgment, which contravene acceptable standards of practice. The profession and the employers need to satisfy themselves that the relevant ethical codes, policies and decision criteria were followed, and they are able to invoke well established disciplinary procedures that include investigation of the circumstances, censure and dismissal. Criminal prosecution may even follow a finding of negligence. However, is it the role of public inquiries, in the form that we have known them, to investigate for disciplinary purposes? If so, can they do so effectively? There clearly has been considerable variance on this issue among panel members and between chairs of inquiries and also, one suspects, conflict between commissioning bodies and the panels. The Tyra Henry report comments that:

> more than once during the inquiry we felt that one limb or other of the council was showing unconcealed pique at the fact that we were not doing what it thought we ought to be doing.[34]

The Lucie Gates inquiry, which nearly floundered because of disagreement about the adversarial process, had been preceded by criticisms and counter-criticisms between local professionals, and the chair reflected that:

> I was left in no doubt that it was hoped by the social and health workers first that we would vindicate them and second that we would make suggestions for improving the system. I do not think that we were an appropriate forum to do either.[35]

Many inquiry panels have particularly stressed that they did not envisage their tasks as including allocation of blame: for example, Karen Spencer, Doreen Aston and Tyra Henry.[36] However, in his review of our book, Sir Louis Blom-Cooper writes:

> The authors fail to understand the nature and purpose of a public inquiry. Inquiries are distinctly not designed to learn constructively from the tragedy, at least not primarily.... Inquiries are formed deliberately by their sponsoring bodies ... to discover what happened, why it happened and *who was responsible* for the happening [our emphasis].[37]

We would contend that this is singularly unclear and that many participants in inquiries over the years have not understood their deliberate purpose to be allocation of responsibility. In our opinion, although public accountability is essential, the nature, process and context of child abuse inquiries makes them an ill-equipped and extremely cumbersome means of achieving this end. What is more concerning is that there has been ambiguity in panels' terms of reference and lack of consensus among leading players as to their contribution to disciplinary measures.

Even if it were clear, this would lead to further problems. First, the emotive context of public inquiries must colour in some way the critical deliberations of the panels. As we discuss more fully below, the public react to tragedies by looking for someone to blame and the media both reflect and encourage this. For instance, after the Hillsborough disaster, a newspaper printed a photograph of a policeman under the headlines: 'This Is The Man Who Opened The Gates' and the photograph of Kimberley Carlile's social worker was reproduced alongside the sub-heading: 'He Let Her Die'. There is enormous pressure to simplify the issues and allocate blame to one or a small number of directly involved personnel. We discern the compulsion to discipline someone as a potent force in the Kimberley Carlile inquiry, which to all outside observers with whom have discussed the case, did not appear to do justice to the social worker criticised. In this case at least, then, professionals have no confidence in the inquiry process as a disciplining measure.

Secondly, no one can learn when they are under threat of disciplinary measures, nor can they contribute to a learning process. When under censure, you make every effort to defend yourself: you take on a guarded demeanour and are circumspect in your answers; you select what information you disclose; you are cautious not to reveal anything that might be misconstrued or used against you; you employ an advocate to emphasise your point of view. These are the opposite stances from those required by a learning exercise, in which one must be free to reveal personal thoughts, information that only you might hold, and explore different hypotheses *without fear of criticism*.

Learning

Professionals have a strong desire to improve their effectiveness and there is usually a wish for all inquiries to highlight lessons that could improve the practice and organisation of child protection work. Inquiries provide opportunities to address such skills as interviewing families, assessing their dynamics, organising information, appraising risk, recognising warning signs, communicating with others, and so on, and in many cases these lessons are at least as important as the policy ones. If mistakes are being repeated in the cases that come to inquiry, then perhaps the wrong lessons are being addressed or the implementation of policy recommendations and their training implications need much greater attention.

In addition, the difficulty we experienced in obtaining the 35 reports for the *Beyond Blame* project illustrates that the conclusions of inquiry panels are not readily available to practitioners, while their format often renders the important lessons inaccessible. Preliminary impressions from our analysis of Department of Health 'Section 8' case reviews is that the review teams were most concerned with whether their child protection procedures were followed, while we are picking up very worrying problems with professionals' assessment skills and thresholds of concern.

The question remains, though, whether inquiries are intended as opportunities for learning. We see in Sir Louis Blom-Cooper's comments above that a leading figure in the field does not think that learning is their main purpose, yet many others have assumed that it is. So, here again, we have ambiguity about the very context of the proceedings.

Catharsis

A child's death at the hands of its parents has been described as 'unimaginable' because it shatters our most fundamental assumptions about human nature and expectations that a helpless young person will be nurtured and protected by its parent/s.[38] Should the possibility of such a catastrophe ever enter public awareness, then the natural wish is for someone to be there to prevent it. In a sense, the hope for a universal rescuer of the helpless and needy represents everyone's infantile fear of dangers in the world and belief that they will find protection and safety. News of a child abuse death is therefore an extremely emotive event, with highly charged feelings of despair for the child, fear of the perpetrator(s)' destructiveness, and impotent rage at 'the someone' who did not rescue. The term 'moral panic' has been used for society's reaction,[39] but we do not think that this is a particularly helpful description.

The media's sensationalist and provocative reporting of child abuse tragedies is well known,[40] but should not be surprising in the light of the emotiveness of the topic. The various feelings need a focus and this is provided by any criminal trial of the parents and then by an inquiry into the work of the professionals. Indeed, many of the inquiries were set up in response to public concern, expressed via the media, politicians or judges. When the public read impassioned reporting of inquiries, it acts as a cathartic experience, allowing expression of powerful fears and emotions.

On the other hand, many people feel enraged by extremes of press reporting and their highly charged writing about tragic cases. It seems to encourage both the primitive emotions and the wish to find someone to blame so that these uncomfortable feelings can be expelled from public consciousness. The danger is that public tolerance for the complexity of the problems is undermined and they are reduced to simple slogans, with the parents cast as demons and the professionals as negligent. If this cathartic experience for society becomes focussed on the inquiry, it is likely to interfere with any learning and disciplinary intentions. In addition, of course, there is little possibility that the inquiry will provide a forum for constructive catharsis for the professionals involved in the case or for relatives of the child victim.

It should be remembered that strong feelings are not just experienced by the public but also by the involved professionals, who can be persecuted by self-blame. Our thinking about reviews has been influenced by consultations with professionals who wished to learn from their own cases of serious injury to, or death of, a child. We undertook these quite independently of each other and it was only in coming together to write the paper for the seminar day, and subsequently this chapter, that we discovered very similar experiences. We each had tried to moderate groups of staff involved in such cases in order to extract lessons from them but, despite very careful preparation, found the atmosphere becoming progressively more highly charged as the cathartic needs surfaced and overtook everything else.

Reassurance

The fourth possible purpose of an inquiry is to restore society's confidence in its public representatives. When politicians, judges or senior administrators call for an inquiry this helps reassure the public that its servants are indeed accountable and that its representatives regard problems of child abuse with equal horror and will address them on society's behalf.

However, it has been suggested that inquiries are called for as a means of political expediency, to demonstrate control and composure and to confine the exploration to a small number of issues.[41]

Recent trends

We may have given an impression that child abuse inquiries to date have shown a degree of consistency in panel composition, procedures and reporting style. However, this is far from the case. Some have been commissioned by central government, others locally; some have been brief ACPC reflections on the case, others major publications which include reviews of the relevant literature; some have been formal and quasi-litigious, others more informal and inquisitorial. Particularly striking has been the absence of an explicit theoretical framework within which to understand the phenomena being investigated.

Nonetheless, there have been significant trends over the two decades since the Maria Colwell inquiry shook the system. Inquiries now tend to be set up locally rather than centrally and to deliberate in private rather than in public. The local agencies sometimes commission an independent body, such as the Bridge Child Care Consultancy Service[42] or respected outside experts,[43] and these panels are much more concerned to extract practical lessons from the tragedies than to accuse professionals of negligence.

The revised *Working Together* guidance crystallised these

trends in Part 8 of the document headed 'Case Reviews'.[44] When abuse is confirmed or suspected as the cause of a child's death, or child protection issues are likely to be a major public concern, each local agency is now required to instigate its own review, to be followed by a composite review by the ACPC. This overview report is then forwarded to the Department of Health and should indicate whether there are any aspects of the case which seem to justify further inquiry, either under the auspices of the ACPC or by an individual agency or agencies. Here the guidance ends, leaving open the possibility that a small number of cases could arouse such attention that the public soul-searching and acrimonious events of old become reinstated.

Nonetheless, the *Working Together* guidance is a welcome development, since it encourages the possibility of local learning from individual cases, with central consideration of policy. However, preliminary impressions from our review of these 'Section 8' reports are that crucial lessons about assessment and appraisal of risk are still not being highlighted because the information has remained unintegrated. In our view, this is the area that needs the greatest attention over the next few years.

A proposed model

When child protection fails, then there are diverse issues which must be addressed. The most important are consideration as to whether workers were negligent, reflection on any lessons to be learned from the case, reassurance that the state monitors such events and opportunities for catharsis. As we have argued, each of these is important, but cannot be satisfied together through a single inquiry. Instead, we would like to propose a slightly different process that separates out each requirement and, we hope, would do justice to each one (see figure 3).

First, the cathartic needs should be addressed, and for professionals we would like to see counselling offered to all involved staff, which would be available to them as individuals and, possibly later, in groups within or across agencies. The counselling need not be prolonged, but should be available for as long as each worker felt the need. It also must be confidential and independent of any inquiry into that person's work on the case.

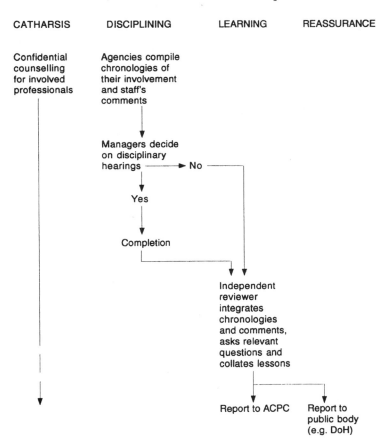

Figure 3. Proposed course of action following a child abuse death or serious injury.

The emotional needs of siblings and other relatives would be met by referral to mental health professionals.[45]

At the same time, we propose that managers within respective agencies bring together information about their staff's involvement in the case in the form of a chronology of events. This would become the material upon which they decide whether there are any disciplinary issues and, if so, this would need to be addressed and completed before any learning is attempted.

Once disciplinary matters are out of the way, potential lessons can be considered. An independent reviewer or reviewers, external to the local system, would be appointed. They would be experienced practitioners in the field of child protection who can articulate a framework within which the events might be understood. They would receive the agencies' chronologies, together with any comments or issues that the practitioners wish to raise, and would integrate the individual accounts into a composite chronology of the whole case. They should have the powers to challenge the submitted accounts and ask additional questions of anyone, including the relatives, if that better enables them to understand the events. They would then compile a report identifying the lessons. This report would be received by the ACPC, who would have responsibility for disseminating the findings in an accessible form in order to address the local practice issues, including training requirements.

The report would also be received and considered by a public body, such as the Department of Health. A summary of the local and central lessons would be made public but, in our view, the prior deliberations are best held in private. Of course, the results of any disciplinary hearings would also be made public.

A scheme such as this need not be expensive of time or resources and could satisfy all the major agendas without one overriding the other. Finally, learning should not only be based on cases which have 'gone wrong', but on work which has gone well or raises matters for debate. This is where the case audit process comes into its own, and we have seen a valuable experiment in one borough. At intervals, a case was chosen for discussion by professionals across agencies which raised interesting issues about child protection. The convener first asked involved workers to name the issues they wished to consider through the case – it might be thresholds of concern, or risk assessment, for example – and then the evolution of the case was presented, with pauses for discussion at any point that seemed pertinent. A summary of the lessons were circulated to the ACPC members for discussion within their own agencies.

Conclusions

Child abuse inquiries have a longer history than those into adult homicide and we have come along way in the last two decades, with many important lessons learned, albeit the hard way, to the benefit of child protection practice. The inquiry process has continued to change, but still leaves room for improvement. We have proposed a scheme that could address all aspects of a case and allow further lessons to emerge, especially in the areas of practical skills and decision taking.

Notes

1. A series of child abuse tragedies leading to Inquiry Reports are referred to in this chapter. By date of publication between 1973 and 1995 the reports are as follows:

Inquiry Report (1973) *Report of Inquiry into the Circumstances Surrounding the Death of Graham Bagnall (D.O.B. 20/5/1970) and the Role of the County Council's Social Services*, Shropshire County Council.

Inquiry Report (1974) *Report of the Committee of Inquiry into the Care and Supervision Provided in Relation to Maria Colwell*, London, HMSO.

Inquiry Report (1978) *Report by Professor J.D. McClean Concerning Karen Spencer to the Derbyshire County Council and Derbyshire Health Authority*, Derbyshire County Council and Derbyshire Health Authority.

Inquiry Report (1982) *Report of Panel of Inquiry*, London Borough of Bexley and Bexley Health Authority.

Inquiry Report (1985) *A Child in Trust: The Report of the Panel of Inquiry into the Circumstances Surrounding the Death of Jasmine Beckford*, London Borough of Brent.

Inquiry Report (1987a) *A Child in Mind: Protection of Children in a Responsible Society. The Report of the Commission of Inquiry into the Circumstances Surrounding the Death of Kimberley Carlile*, London Borough of Greenwich.

Inquiry Report (1987b) *Whose Child? The Report of the Public Inquiry into the Death of Tyra Henry*, London Borough of Lambeth.

Inquiry Report (1989) *The Doreen Aston Report*, Lewisham Social Services.

Inquiry Report (1990) *The Report of the Stephanie Fox Practice Review*, Wandsworth Area Child Protection Committee.

Inquiry Report (1991) *Sukina: An Evaluation of the Circumstances Leading to Her Death*, The Bridge Child Care Consultancy Service.

Inquiry Report (1995) *Paul: Death Through Neglect*, The Bridge Child Care Consultancy Service.

2. See Creighton S.J. (1992) *Child Abuse Trends in England and Wales 1988-1990: And an Overview from 1973-1990*, London, NSPCC; and James G. (1994) *Study of Working Together 'Part 8' Reports*, Department of Health.

3. Home Office, Department of Health, Department of Education and Science, and Welsh Office (1991) *Working Together under the Children Act 1989: A Guide to Arrangements for Inter-agency Co-operation for the Protection of Children from Abuse*, London, HMSO.

4. Home Office (1945) *Report by Sir Walter Monkton KCMG, KCVO, MC, KC, on the Circumstances which Led to the Boarding Out of Denis and Terrance O'Neill at Bank Farm, Minsterley, and the Steps Taken to Supervise their Welfare*, London, HMSO.

5. Inquiry Report (1973) op. cit., Inquiry Report (1974) op. cit.

6. Reder P., Duncan S. and Gray M. (1993a) *Beyond Blame: Child Abuse Tragedies Revisited*, London, Routledge.

7. See, for example, Butler-Sloss E. (1988) *Report of the Inquiry into Child Abuse in Cleveland 1987*, London, HMSO; and Clyde J.J. (1992) *The Report of the Inquiry into the Removal of Children from Orkney in February 1991*, Edinburgh, HMSO.

8. Figure 1 is reproduced from Reder, Duncan and Gray (1993a) op. cit., at p. 156 and Figure 2 adapted from the same source at p. 139. See also generally McGoldrick M. and Gerson R. (1985) *Genograms in Family Assessment*, New York, Norton.

9. Reder P., Duncan S. and Gray M. (1993b) 'A new look at child abuse tragedies', *Child Abuse Review* 2, 89-100; Reder P., Duncan S. and Gray M. (1993c) 'Child protection dilemmas in a "not-existing" pattern of abuse', *Journal of Family Therapy* 15, 57-64; and Reder P. and Duncan S. (in press) 'Closure, covert warnings and escalating child abuse', *Child Abuse and Neglect*.

10. Reder, Duncan and Gray (1993a) op. cit.

11. See Parton N. (1981) 'Child abuse, social anxiety and welfare', *British Journal of Social Work* 11, 391-414; and Howitt D. (1992) *Child Abuse Errors: When Good Intentions Go Wrong*, Hemel Hempstead, Harvester Wheatsheaf.

12. Adcock M. (1989) Presentation to the Institute of Family Therapy conference *Child Care and the State*, London, June; Hill M. (1990) 'The manifest and latent lessons of child abuse inquiries', *British Journal of Social Work* 20, 197-213.

13. Inquiry Report (1974) op. cit.

14. Inquiry Report (1987a) op. cit.

15. Hallett C. and Birchall E. (1992) *Co-ordination and Child Protection: A Review of the Literature*, Edinburgh, HMSO.

16. Inquiry Report (1985) op. cit.

17. Hallett C. and Stevenson O. (1980) *Child Abuse: Aspects of Interprofessional Co-operation*, London, George Allen and Unwin.

18. Creighton (1992) op. cit.

19. Inquiry Reports 1985, 1987b and 1987a respectively, op. cit.

20. See Creighton (1992) op. cit.

21. Hallett C. (1989) 'Child abuse inquiries and public policy' in O. Stevenson (ed.) *Child Abuse: Public Policy and Professional Practice*, Hemel Hempstead: Harvester Wheatsheaf.

22. Dingwall R. (1986) 'The Jasmine Beckford affair', *Modern Law Review* 49, 489-507.

23. Hallett (1989) op. cit.

24. Inquiry Report (1982) op. cit.

25. Inquiry Report (1987b) op. cit. at 161

26. Reder, Duncan and Gray (1993a) op. cit.

27. Morris P. (1987) 'Counting the cost of child abuse inquiries', *Community Care*, November 26, 7.

28. See, for example, Fontana, V. and Alfaro J. (1987) *High Risk Factors Associated with Child Maltreatment Fatalities*, New York: Mayor's Task Force on Child Abuse and Neglect; Dingwall R. (1989) 'Some problems about predicting child abuse and neglect' in O. Stevenson (ed.) *Child Abuse: Public Policy and Professional Practice*, Hemel Hempstead, Harvester Wheatsheaf; Hallett and Birchall (1992) op. cit.; and Browne K. (1995) 'Predicting maltreatment' in P. Reder and C. Lucey (eds) *Assessment of Parenting: Psychiatric and Psychological Contributions*, London, Routledge.

29. Hutchinson R. (1986) 'The effect of inquiries into cases of child abuse upon the social work profession', *British Journal of Criminology* 26, 178-82.

30. Section 8 reviews are discussed in Home Office *et al.* (1991) op. cit.

31. See, for example, Morris P. (1975) 'The question the Aukland inquiry dodged', *Community Care* December 10, 18-19; Mawby R., Fisher C. and Hale J. (1979) 'The press and Karen Spencer', *Social Work Today* 10, 22, 13-16; Raymond B. (1987) 'A child abuse inquiry – the lawyer's tale', *Social Work Today*, December 7, 16-17; and Ruddock M. (1987) 'A child abuse inquiry – the social worker's tale', *Social Work Today*, December 7, 14-15.

32. Shearer A. (1979) 'The legacy of Maria Colwell', *Social Work Today* 10, 19, 12-19; and Hutchinson (1986) op. cit.

33. Inquiry Report (1987b) op. cit., at 3.

34. Ibid., at 159

35. Inquiry Report (1982) op. cit., at Vol. 1: Chairman's Report, Appendix VII, p. xxviii.

36. Inquiry Reports 1978, 1989 and 1987b respectively, op. cit.

37. Blom-Cooper L. (1994) 'Book review', *Criminal Behaviour and Mental Health* 4 (Book Review Supplement to No. 4) 109-10.

38. Geraldine Fitzpatrick, personal communication.

39. See, for example, Parton (1981) op. cit.

40. See, for example, Mawby *et al.* (1979) op. cit.; and Donaldson L.J.

and O'Brien S. (1995) 'Press coverage of the Cleveland child sexual abuse enquiry: a source of public enlightenment?', *Journal of Public Health Medicine* 17, 70-6.

   41. See, for example, Hallett (1989) op. cit.
   42. See Inquiry Report (1991) and (1995) op. cit.
   43. Inquiry Report (1990) op. cit.
   44. Home Office *et al.* (1991) op. cit.
   45. Reder P. and Fitzpatrick G. (in press) 'Assessing the needs of siblings following a child abuse death', *Child Abuse Review*.

The Inquiry and Victims' Families

Paul Rock

This is a first, tentative attempt to make sense of material that I am still gathering, through interview, observation and reading, on organizations established to support and campaign for families bereaved by homicide, principally SAMM (Support After Murder and Manslaughter, formerly Parents of Murdered Children); but also Justice for Victims, the Zito Trust, Disaster Action, the Suzy Lamplugh Trust, Families of Murdered Children, RoadPeace, Victims' Voice and others. Those I have spoken to have played a key part in that history, and everyone has lost children or close relatives through murder or manslaughter. They tend to call themselves the 'secondary victims' of murder, personal bereavement being a precondition of full membership, and they call their organizations the groups that no one wishes to join.

It should be emphasized that my work is centred on the history of a very particular set of political and practical responses. It is in effect an academic study of organizing as a mode of survival, and the result has been to steer analysis in a number of obvious and less-than-obvious ways. First, the homicides that prompted the responses were known and mourned by survivors who cared enough to do something about them, and not all victims and missing persons are thus mourned (indeed numbers of missing persons simply 'disappear' each year and no one searches for them). Secondly, the homicides were regarded by the bereaved as uncommon and shocking: none seemed to have occurred within social groups bearing what Wolfgang and Ferracuti once called a 'subculture of violence',[1] groups where woundings, assaults and injuries are commonplace and perhaps not very shocking at all (indeed there were apprehensions in one self-help group that they might have to admit the family of someone killed in a vendetta between criminal gangs, but that did not come to pass). Thirdly, I have focused quite strictly on survivors in their role as organizers, and on organizing as a symbolic and pragmatic process, rather than on the bereaved as a general category. Fourthly, I did not address the specific issue of inquiries until I was invited to do so for this paper. Fifthly, I write descriptively rather than prescriptively, striving merely to grasp and reproduce the views of victims' families. And, lastly, it should be noted that it seems to be the extraordinary murder, the murder with unusual consequences or, perhaps, the unusual survivor that will lead to the taking of exceptional action, to campaigning, the founding of self-help groups, and the memorialisation of victims in trusts and groups bearing their name. The more extensive experiences of the wider population of those bereaved by homicide have necessarily been pushed to the margins of analysis.

Homicide and bereavement

Those I have met cannot perhaps be considered 'typical' secondary victims, and the homicides which so distressed them were not quite characteristic of murder and manslaughter in the United Kingdom. Only one of the main people I interviewed had been touched by what is known as a 'domestic murder'[2] although 25 per cent of the total population of male victims of homicide and 60 per cent of female victims are likely to be murdered in this manner in England and Wales each year. (Domestic murder may, of course, be even more distressing and confusing in its consequences than murder committed by an outsider or stranger: it may give rise to torn loyalties and sympathies, a compounded sense of guilt, and obstacles to the formation of unambiguous symbolic, emotional and moral responses. Voluntary organizations for the bereaved have had their difficulties in accepting and assimilating people so affected, just as they have had their forebodings about the implications of supporting the criminal families of the violent victim.)

Wolfgang,[3] Polk,[4] Luckenbill[5] and others have reminded us that most murders are the outcome of an acrimonious relationship, a violent social world or a dangerous life-style. The homicides they describe were committed by women against their male partners in the kitchen or by men against their female partners in the bedroom; and by inebriated males against other young males in bars, pubs and streets. If I spoke to no one mourning an ordinary domestic murder, there were certainly examples of killings in pubs and streets, and their deaths were seen to be an abrupt, casual and meaningless waste of life which bewildered and confounded those who had been left behind.

Some of the homicides I learned about were particularly savage or shocking. Others had become ensnared in administrative and legal entanglements at a time when people were least able to contend with them (both the founders of Parents of Murdered Children, for example, lost children in countries overseas and were obliged to negotiate with foreign police forces, courts and officials for information and the return of the bodies). Others still had been mismanaged by prosecuting or investigating authorities, leading to the frustrations of botched trials or unexplained and seemingly inexplicable changes of charge or plea.

Murder brings in its train multiple problems for the living which must be described before the sentiments and wishes of 'secondary victims of homicide' become more intelligible.[6] I shall proceed by constructing a brief, impressionistic, ideal-type, distilled from the work I have undertaken so far, condensed and exaggerated for analytic effect, and devised to answer the questions before the seminar and posed again in this book. If I write somewhat graphically it is because I have tried to remain true to the phenomenon, and what I am seeking to recreate is itself as intense as any experience can be. It is what psychiatrists would call a normal reaction to abnormal events and SAMM would prefer to call a natural reaction to highly unnatural circumstances. It is not a pathological response, but certainly one beyond the range of understanding of those who have not experienced it, and therefore alienating and difficult to comprehend. Although the ideal-type might not cover homicide survivors at large, it may be of use in discussing the kinds of problem that require the intercession of an inquiry. It should certainly fit some aspects of the Jason Mitchell case.

The *Shorter Oxford English Dictionary* defines bereavement as being, *inter alia,* robbed, stripped, dispossessed and left desolate, and that captures much of the experience. Bereavement is generally harrowing, but it is yet more harrowing still after homicide.[7] Killing performed by an outsider can rarely be anticipated, it is an appalling and untoward act in most parts of the United Kingdom, and the unpredicted death is more shocking than the loss for which there can be a measure of preparation.[8] It is marked by violence and intentionality or by wantonness and irrationality: someone manifestly *wanted* the victim to die or behaved as if he were indifferent to the consequences. Death thus arising could have been otherwise. It could have been prevented. And those who are killed are often young, dead before their time and in defiance of the natural order. One meaning of victim, again derived from the *Shorter Oxford English Dictionary*, is a person 'who is reduced or destined to suffer under some oppressive or destructive agency'. The family may indeed experience that oppressiveness and destructiveness. They and the victim were powerless to prevent what occurred, and powerlessness rankles. It belittles and emasculates them.

It is difficult to justify such deaths as timely, inevitable, orderly or necessary. There are no comforting words of that sort to be invoked. They are the very opposite of the 'good death', and responses to them are correspondingly acute.

The immediate reaction to murder is almost invariably rank disbelief.[9] Murder is conceived to be so improbable, unplanned and devastating that many families manifest a blank refusal to admit what has occurred. Over and again they will say 'this can't be happening to us. It's all a bad dream' (even in America, where the homicide rate is appreciably greater than that of the United Kingdom, where murder is not really very uncommon, murder tends to be regarded as 'a foreign, frightening event in the lives of unfortunate others'[10]). The bereaved may withdraw to become mute[11] and immobile, unprepared at first to accept what they have been told. Thereafter, theirs can be a compound of profoundly distressing emotions of anger, pain and loss, a kind of experiential chaos in which there is a collapse of the structures that once sustained their personal and social lives. They will have no guiding scripts, models or mentors for behaviour, no signs about what to do next, no expectations about what may yet come, no good purpose in life. On the contrary, lacking familiar recipes for action, survivors confront what sociologists call *anomie*. Berger and Luckman argued:

> The legitimation of the institutional order ... is faced with the ongoing necessity of keeping chaos at bay. *All* social reality is precarious. *All* societies are constructed in the face of chaos. The constant possibility of anomic terror is actualized whenever the legitimations that obscure the precariousness are threatened or collapse.[12]

Berger and Luckman offer bereavement as just such an example of anomic terror. Meaning is lost,[13] and the secondary victims of homicide can retreat into a private grief so deep and ineffable that they risk estrangement even from those close to them, from others who are also grieving, endangering the very fabric of their close social world. Bereavement after homicide can be corrosive and isolating, throwing members of families and social networks in on themselves in a kind of implosion of anguish. At its very core, there is a mass of confusing, frightening and tumultuous sensations which propel people step by step and often blindly. The word used most frequently to describe those feelings is *anger*, although it may be conjectured that anger is only an approximate, and perhaps not even a very appropriate, term for a much more complicated, turbulent and inchoate state of mind and body. Those feelings can be turned inwards to promote withdrawal, depression or suicide; outwards to constitute what would be called 'stridency' by insiders working in and about the criminal justice system,[14] and the voice of authentic grief by the campaigner; or become transmuted to energise processes of constructing organizations and supporting others.[15] In two of those modes may be seen a practical attempt to experience oneself as a person with agency, as one who can act on the world rather than be acted upon, in a symbolic denial of powerlessness. (Any one person may, of course, pass in and out of those different forms of experience, sometimes melding them in new combinations.)

There is no one formula for experiencing and displaying intense grief. Although its various constituent acts and symbols are drawn from the currency of everyday life, it is behaviour that can never be well-rehearsed, smoothly-performed or wholly coherent, and much has become private for want of public conventions appropriate to the situation. Grief has its contradictions. Indeed, the control of extreme emotion may itself be problematic: to regulate it would imply that it lacked spontaneity, not to regulate it would transform it into a source of embarrassment and public discomfiture, and, more difficult still, the very question of how it is to be identified can become a source of anxiety. A frequent question asked by the bereaved is 'Is this normal? Am I going mad?' One of the comforts self-help groups provide is the reassurance that such extreme reactions are indeed normal.

Many will bear their pain with outward fortitude but they can suffer in diverse ways within. Some people will carry on with mundane activities in an effort to reassert structure or for want of anything better to do, but others may cease to care about them altogether: such activities may indeed lose all apparent objective, especially when they once centred on or embraced the victim. The bereaved may no longer wish to work or to care for themselves and their possessions. Indeed, to do otherwise for some could be read falsely as a reversion to the everyday world, as an end to mourning and a return to normality that imply, as they would say, that they have 'moved on'. 'Moving on' for the heavily traumatised would signify a consent to forgetfulness and emotional negligence amounting to what would be considered a betrayal of the victim,[16] and pride may be taken in a conspicuous neglect of the routine demands of ordinary life. A very few practise a form of deep mourning akin symbolically to the rending of clothes and smearing of ashes.

For a long while, the bereaved will be transfixed by that one awful phenomenon of murder. It will dominate their thoughts, displacing almost everything else, feeding recurrent nightmares; inducing illness, irritability and bodily palpitations; and exciting feelings of vulnerability, a suspiciousness of strangers, fears about leaving the home or travelling on public transport. They will be loath to read newspapers or watch television because the media are replete with images and reports of violent death. Other children may effectively have to forfeit their own childhood as their parents brood about the absent victim (one woman said, rather ashamed, 'I look at him [her surviving child] and sometimes wish it was ―――― [her murdered son]'). Businesses can decline or become bankrupt. The bereaved may be dismissed from employment. Time will appear to stand still, practically irrelevant after the one huge, overshadowing, traumatic event of murder,[17] no longer measured by conventional clock or public calendar but by a new timetable of birthdays, anniversaries, Christmas and New Year focused on intimate events in the past lives of family and victim. The victims' bedrooms and possessions may be left untouched, cleaned but otherwise intact, a visible sign that their owners have not been forgotten, that they remain present symbolically. Relations with neighbours, friends and relatives can become strained as others appear blithely to go about their everyday affairs in a setting that has changed so tragically and irreversibly for the secondary victims. The bereaved sense themselves to be out of joint, strangers to the commonplace world, emotionally alienated.

Accompanying that shock and dissociation there may be other confounding emotions with a power to bewilder and hurt. In the wake of a killing, acquaintances or members of the family may have simultaneously and hastily to reappraise their knowledge about the victim. In the case of adolescent victims, for example, Riley and Shaw[18] and Maung[19] reveal that many parents do not know, cannot control and are not always told a great deal about their children's behaviour outside the house. On occasion, but certainly not invariably, the shock of learning about a child's death will be exacerbated by the discovery of new and disagreeable facts about his or her associates and style of life. Thus, one bereaved mother was dismayed to learn that her son had been killed by someone purporting to be a dealer as he had sought to buy drugs. Surviving members of the family may then encounter a new confusion, finding it hard to assemble what they most fervently seek, an unsullied memory, just when that memory is about to be fixed and retained. They may experience remorse and guilt about the things that were left undone and unsaid and the things that should have been done and said, about unresolved quarrels and unmet promises. They may experience guilt that they survived although the victim did not.

For a long while, the one object that commands their interest is the life and death of the victim. When the victim is young (as they so often are in instances when the bereaved campaign or support one another) there will be a knowledge of how much was incomplete in his or her life, how much 'unfinished business' there was.[20] They will talk urgently and incessantly about little else, trying, as it were, to resurrect and hold his or her memory in conversation, trying to make sense of what can be ascertained, often to the point of estranging friends and relatives who may wish to discuss other matters, or divert them in the hope that they will 'move on'. They will have a need for information about what happened, demanding to know every detail in a profound craving to understand causes and reasons (one father said to me of the deaths of his son and daughter-in-law, 'there was no way they were going to put them underground and make them into a statistic. I had to know what had happened'). They will explore troubling hypotheses about what *might* have happened had they themselves behaved differently (known as the 'if only' problem): could death have been averted had they or others known more, done more, or been elsewhere? They will search for signs of some larger purpose in what occurred lest they succumb to moral nihilism. Arbitrary and cruel crime is a denial of the presumption of a just world, that right doing will lead to proper desserts, that virtue will be rewarded and sin punished. Might it be possible to discover actions and justifications that could restore moral significance and proportion to life?

An unremitting, diffuse anger will at first fuel questions and criticisms (but not always or in every case) about the crime and the murderer, and about the secondary victims' treatment by the press, Victim Support, psychiatrists, counsellors, the Crown Prosecution Service and the criminal justice system (the police tend exceptionally to be singled out for praise). A member of one group said, 'I don't trust authority any more. There's so much corruption out there.' They will search for pattern, causality and intelligibility. They will ask a chain of questions: what really happened, why did matters go wrong, what would have happened, 'if only' something different had been done? And the ensuing answer is very likely to refract the intensity of that anger and the urgency of the need to know. It will often be couched in a language of accountability which assigns personal blame for misfortune[21] (one man said, 'the one question I was really interested in was who was responsible for the decision to release him' – the killer from a special hospital). Drabeck and Quarantelli once argued:

> Disasters can ... evoke ... a relentless search for scapegoats to blame for destruction and loss of life. This tendency to seek the cause in a *who* – rather than a *what* – is common after airplane crashes, fires, cave-ins, and other catastrophes .... Personalizing blame in this way is ... a standard response ....[22]

Out of that struggle for meaning in the midst of an initial chaos may emerge a potent new symbolic order which does not and cannot recapitulate the organization of mundane experience before trauma, although it may itself shift and weaken over time. Not unlike other situations in which disorder is superseded and transformed,[23] an initial confusion can give way through charged feeling to narratives organized around sets of highly-coloured antitheses, to strong moral and figurative contrasts between innocence and sin, blamelessness and blameworthiness, the good and the bad, the friend who is an ally and the enemy who conspires against one.

In one important instance, it is tempting to capture the formulation of oppositions in the language of Jungian archetypes[24] or Lévi-Strauss's structuralism, although my invocation of such imagery here is at best convenient and metaphorical and will demand more rigorous analysis at a later stage.

Jung talked about the archetypes as fundamental symbolic processes within the self. Lévi-Strauss talked about binary oppositions as a linguistic device with which to analyse the organization of social structure. I take it that it is those phenomena and processes, or ones very similar in structure and function, that infuse relations as symbolic chaos gives way to order after murder.

In the aftermath of homicide, it is as if there were a reversion to a more elemental mode of symbolisation in which victim and offender are, on occasion, reconstructed and objectified within the allegorical system of the bereaved and extended out to become the victim and the murderer, the self and its shadow, tied in a dialectical bond. Victim and offender are interdependent oppositions: one predicates the other, the character of the one informs the other, the fate of the one is contrasted continually with the fate of the other: the murderer lives, the victim does not (one mother of a murdered daughter was overheard to say that 'He got life. It's too good for him. He's still breathing'); the murderer has a future, the victim has no future; the murderer is active, the victim immobile; the murderer is guilty, the victim innocent; the murderer is bad, the victim good (a member of one organization said to me: 'The victims I'm told about are always brilliant people, nice people, I don't know why'); the murderer is represented in court, the victim is not; the murderer's story and character are laid before the court, the victim's are not; the murderer has a defined place in the ecology of the courtroom and courthouse, the victim's family do not (although that is beginning rapidly to change). Out of greyness and confusion thereby emerge twin, polarised images of evil and virtue, images that are underscored most poignantly in the small domestic shrine, ornamented with candles, photographs and flowers, that is often prepared for the victim.[25]

Homicide survivors are divided, as we all are, about the efficacy and propriety of different forms of punishment. Many are remarkably free of retributive sentiments, but, if only for a while, they do tend to interpret the world within a frame set by that symbiotic relation. The lot of the murderer and the lot of the victim are symbolically linked: doing something to the murder can, by analogical reasoning, do something to the victim. The way in which the murderer is treated bears heavily on how the victim is thought to be regarded. By extension too, the way in which they, the victim's surrogate, are treated, reflects on the victim and the murderer. A leaflet for SAMM Merseyside demands:

> We are aware of those organisations who offer help to offenders, ex-offenders and their families .... How many organisations can you think of that offer help to the families of murder victims?

That is the existential core of much bereavement, and it lets loose a mass of new sensitivities that amplify slights. Many survivors were incensed that trials were conducted in the name of the defendant rather than that of the victim (victims have no legal standing and very little social standing in the criminal justice system of England and Wales, and murder victims' families are, by and large, even more obscure, being, at best, merely members of 'the public'). They found it intolerable that details of the victim's name or life were misreported by the press or in court. And they did not care for the propensity of others to refrain from discussing the murder or from referring to the victim by name, as if it were better that all memory should be expunged, as if the victim had become an unperson. One mother told me: 'You do have to speak up for your child, and you do have to regain your memory.'

Those sensitivities were alerted repeatedly in the confusing *sequelae* to murder. Many of those I met had had to confront the unexpected proclivity of investigating officers to look upon *them* as suspects in the first instance, that is, for police support to be tinged with suspicion, rendering communication disquietingly ambiguous at a time when it should have been the most transparent, and muddling the moral character of the survivors when it was felt to be most stark. They had faced the loss of a home territory (if the death occurred at home) as it became transformed into a 'crime scene' profoundly violated by death: it had become unexpectedly difficult for them to retreat to a comforting, private place to be on their own. They may have had to face the need eventually to cleanse the home of blood and other harrowing signs of violence, an act that required considerable determination. They may have had difficulties in gaining access to, and control over, the body of a victim now regarded formally as the property of the coroner, just at a time when that access and control have become of paramount symbolic importance, last tokens of concern, and the effect may disable them as mourners.[26] They may have had to deal with the constant curiosity and surveillance of outsiders and a prurient press. They may have encountered rumours and innuendoes in neighbourhood, workplace and courtroom that blamed the victim for somehow provoking or deserving his or her own death (after all, violent death is an uncommon event and, turning to the 'just world' hypothesis, outsiders may well conjecture in their turn that the victim must have 'asked for it'. Defence lawyers and relatives of the accused may be eager to feed those conjectures as *they* attempt to give a sympathetic order and meaning to events. And the dead cannot answer back.) The bereaved may experience a new and often unexpected social isolation as others distance themselves from those now evidently blighted by misfortune.[27] They are those for whom there are no familiar responses, the benighted people who provoke unease and embarrassment instead.

Inquiries after Homicide

How do these observations feed into the matter of 'Inquiries after Homicide'? Louis Blom-Cooper listed four principal functions served by public inquiries: establishing the facts; identification of individual culpability; surveying the arrangements that led to the scandal, disaster or abuse; and holding up to obloquy the actions that threatened public confidence.[28] Those are all purposes which many bereaved families (and indeed the families of murderers[29]) may also be expected to support, but it is evident that they would look to tribunals for other ends as well. I consulted individuals and members of Disaster Action, Justice for Victims, the Suzy Lamplugh Trust, Support After Murder and Manslaughter and the Zito Trust before writing this chapter. Above all, I am grateful to the son and daughter of the Wilsons who spoke to me about the murder of their parents and its aftermath. Their views are especially valuable in the context of this book.

Individuals and groups differ in their judgements and wishes: some are more considered than others; some are more conversant with tribunal and legal procedures than others; and some have greater access to lawyers and psychiatrists. Particularly important are the relations which members of a family establish with those who can offer assistance and information. There is the problem that, in their understandable appetite for knowledge, and particularly in the aftermath of a terrible death, no court, committee, tribunal or inquiry could ever fully satisfy every family. The matter is yet further complicated when there is a suspicion of 'cover-up' which leads people to mistrust what they are told, surmising that there *must* be more that can be known. And, for those who have been the most severely traumatised, one may suppose, new information might not always be heeded. The awful event of the death and its immediate consequences can block out much that transpires subsequently. Narratives can be littered with allegations and counter-allegations about the neglect of families by the police and Victim Support, for instance. (But, it should be remarked, none of these latter problems seemed to have afflicted the two members of the Wilson family I met. They had been well-supported and informed by Victim Support, SAMM, their solicitor, the secretary of the Independent Inquiry, and, above all, by the police, and they felt they were reasonably knowledgeable about events as they unfolded.)

The following must necessarily again be a simplification of a complex position, it contains propositions to which not every family and group would subscribe, but it not only follows the logic of bereavement as I have described it but also the express views of individuals and campaigning and self-help groups. These other ends would include:

(i) Explaining the functions and workings of inquiries. Like much else, inquiries almost certainly constitute an utterly new and perhaps arcane experience for the bereaved (they may well be the only lay people with an immediate interest in the proceedings) and they hold that it would be of assistance to have procedures, processes and rights explained clearly in advance, perhaps personally (it should be noted that the Home Office's forthcoming 'fact pack' for the bereaved does have a section on Mental Health Review Tribunals). At present, said one person, 'No one takes you through it', and, said another, 'They're not very good in giving you help in asking relevant questions'. Lack of preparatory information can be one more source of confusion among many.

(ii) For practical and symbolic purposes, awarding the families a right to legal representation should they wish to exercise it. Practically, such representation would afford them considerable assistance in the phrasing and putting of questions and in the deciphering of replies. Symbolically, representation would restore to the bereaved the sense that they have been acknowledged (a much used word); that they are also a party to the proceedings, that they have retained some property in a problem that affects them most vitally[30] (a member of one organization I consulted asserted that 'People are made to feel they are wholly irrelevant to the process. They feel ignored.') In effect, representation would help promote the reintegration of a group of people who too often believe themselves to be excluded. A galling contrast may be traced with the treatment afforded the perpetrator who *can* receive legal representation (Jason Mitchell did request, but was refused representation) and, as Jill Peay has reminded me, 'even financial compensation from the authorities for their failure to care, whilst the families are expected to finance their own representation – assuming it is allowed'.

(iii) Permitting survivors to talk formally and publicly at some point about the character and history of the victim and about the impact which his or her death has had upon them ('I want to tell them what we've lost'). Such a measure would be cathartic for many. It is becoming commonplace in many of the courts of North America. It would introduce vicariously and symbolically the one person whom families conceive to be the pivot of deliberations ('I was able to tell them how I feel. The actual victims could not speak for themselves', said one involved in a committee of inquiry into a murder very similar to that committed by Jason Mitchell).

The situation appears unsettled. Jill Peay remarked that 'the role and purpose of the Inquiry has never been definitively clarified. Families recognise the opportunities it presents to explore issues and raise questions denied to them at a "trial", but there is no formal role for them to play at the Inquiry.' In the Lockerbie inquiry, families *were* allowed, as one member stated, to 'say what had happened and what it is like to be on the receiving end. We were allowed to have our say and that was very important.' (The two Wilson family members themselves said that they would have liked to claim that right to say what impact the deaths of their parents had had upon them: 'in the early days I wanted that very strongly. I wanted to say our piece and say what we thought .... It's not about our parents, it's about Jason Mitchell, but it's had an impact on the family. It's affected the whole of the family. People should be aware that it has effects.')

(iv) Divulging in detail whatever can reasonably be ascertained about the events leading up to and culminating in the homicide. Some trials are not contested and the information given will be correspondingly meagre. The trial of Jason Mitchell is an instance: it was not fought and it lasted for less than half a day. All trials rely on edited materials, the 'facts of the case', which do not satisfy the great need of survivors to know and understand what happened. The Inquiry may be the one, final opportunity families have to comprehend how and 'why' the victim was killed. Wherever possible, copies of documents presented to the Inquiry should also be distributed to families if they should wish to have them. Of course, at present, families can receive quite lengthy and courteous replies to questions and points raised, and no case can or should be reported in its totality, but there is a need for information beyond the instrumental requirements of establishing the facts and identifying culpability. At the very least, divulging matters in this way could help to dispel demons. 'I felt for the rest of my life it was something that would be in the back of my mind. If it could be made clearer, I wanted to know,' said Chris Wilson, 'It would just help to understand what happened on the actual day.' And his sister said, 'It does help to put an actual picture to it, because otherwise you fabricate so much .... You picture so many scenarios ....'

(v) Making recommendations that might prevent the repetition of a particular occurrence. There is a repeated demand that others should not experience what the bereaved have 'been through', and preventive measures are of keen interest to them. One person reflected, 'I've said that in my case it's too late, but if I can do anything to prevent it happening again ...', and Chris Wilson himself said that an identification and acknowledgement of structural flaws would be important for the future prevention of other lapses.

(vi) In some instances, making fully accountable those whose decisions or 'non-decisions' led to the death, and, by full accountability, a number of families would intend dismissal, demotion or the making of monetary compensation directly to the families affected. (Personal accountability and blaming were less in the minds of the Wilson family than the need to understand how the system regulating Jason Mitchell's discharge had failed: 'We're not casting blame. We're not pointing our finger at anybody in particular. We want the Inquiry to look at the system, why he was allowed out ....' Indeed, Chris Wilson had told the Inquiry that Jason Mitchell had been 'let down'.)

More specifically, a number of families and organizations would wish Mental Health Review Tribunals and other bodies:

(vii) To consult with the families about the possible impending release of patients, including the right to submit evidence and make representations about their apprehensions of risk.

(viii) To award the right to submit and have considered, in addition to medical evidence, information on the criminal antecedents of patients.

(ix) To introduce greater transparency and openness in proceedings ('it's a closed society'). That the Independent Inquiry should be public was a matter of importance to Chris Wilson and his sister: 'The main reason ... is that it would bring to public attention the reason why the deaths happened. I don't think I know it would change things, but it would bring them to public awareness. At least someone is standing there and saying something has happened and something has gone wrong, and it would it become part of public awareness.'

(x) To enter on police computer records details of potentially dangerous offenders who have not been convicted by reason of insanity so that risks to particular and general members of the public may be lessened.

(xi) To provide feedback to families about specific decisions taken in cases that might affect them and about general changes in law and procedure. People at risk of injury, they would argue, have a right to be warned.

Conclusion

Bereavement in the wake of homicide simultaneously robs the secondary victim of a sense of structure, purpose and moral significance (one said that he had been a 'zombie' for years) and instils a tumult of emotions most commonly described as anger. It is a process profoundly implicated in problems of meaning, and the demands it generates revolve around meaning in their turn. What survivors want is a combination of reforms centred on practical and symbolic matters.

Bereavement alienates survivors from the patterns and preoccupations of everyday life, concentrating their attention urgently on the victim, and on the events and people that contributed to his or her death. It engenders a powerful, near inexhaustible, search for understanding and explanation that would amount, in effect, to a regaining of personal mastery over circumstances so manifestly thrown out of control.

Monetary compensation or retribution are not always principally at issue, although the consequences of death can be expensive and painful. Rather, the search should be seen in part as a quest for a special form of redress to the victims and those who mourn them. There is a need for the reassertion of moral balance that can be achieved only by emphasizing responsibility and accountability when wrongs or mistakes are committed. And there is more involved: it is as if those with responsibility in the criminal justice system and health services should be required to work hard to mark the gravity of the homicide itself, to behave as if they regard murder and manslaughter in a manner considered seemly by the bereaved.

At issue too is a desire to be represented, to be considered formally a participant in procedures that touch their own affairs so closely, to be acknowledged and respected, to be given dignity (all words in common currency among the new groups). There are often sound practical needs behind the demand for representation: the bereaved may be moved by the wish effectively to communicate what is known to them alone; they would wish to learn as much as they can; and most would wish to ensure that what had afflicted them should not afflict others. But there are symbolic demands as well. At stake, it may be supposed, is the analogical reasoning that asserts that recognition of their worth and their right to be accepted may be read as signs of their own emotional investment in the death, the consequentiality of the victim and the suffering that his or her death has wrought.

Acknowledgment

I am grateful to Jane Cooper, co-ordinator of SAMM; Coline Covington; Jill Peay; and Chris Wilson and his sister Catherine, for their comments.

Notes

1. Wolfgang M. and Ferracuti F. (1967) *The Subculture of Violence*, Tavistock.

2. One may surmise that many members of SAMM were the secondary victims of domestic homicide but it is difficult to make a judgement because SAMM does not yet have detailed information about its members.

3. Wolfgang M. (1958) *Patterns of Criminal Homicide*, University of Pennsylvania Press.

4. Polk K. (1994) *When Men Kill: Scenarios of Masculine Violence*, Cambridge University Press.

5. Luckenbill D. (1977) 'Criminal homicide as a situated transaction', *Social Problems* 25, 176-86.

6. A useful collection of American case histories is offered by Magee D. (1983) *What Murder Leaves Behind*, Dodd, Mead and Co.

7. See Green J. and Green M. (1992) *Dealing with Death*, Chapman and Hall, at 125.

8. See Straebe W. and Straebe M. (1987) *Bereavement and Health*, Cambridge University Press, at 207.

9. See Murray Parkes C. (1993) 'Psychiatric problems following bereavement by murder or manslaughter', *British Journal of Psychiatry* 162, at 50.

10. Rynearson E. (1984) 'Bereavement after homicide: a descriptive study', *American Journal of Psychiatry* 141, at 1453.

11. See Marris P. (1986) *Loss and Change*, Routledge and Kegan Paul, at 25.

12. Berger P. and Luckman T. (1967) *The Social Construction of Reality*, Allen Lane, The Penguin Press, at 117.

13. As it tends to be lost in the aftermath of more mundane death. See Mellor P. (1993) 'Death in high modernity', in D. Clark (ed.) *The Sociology of Death*, Blackwell, at 23.

14. See Casey S. (1995) 'Victims' rights', *Oxford Magazine* 7, at 25.

15. See Amick-McMullan A., Kirkpatrick D. and Veronen L. (1989)

'Family survivors of homicide victims: a behavioral analysis', *Behavior Therapist* 12, at 75.

16. Some holocaust survivors have felt a like distress that they and others are beginning to forget what happened in the 1930s and 1940s. Bruno Bettelheim and Primo Levi are perhaps the most prominent recent instances.

17. Almost everyone I spoke with had no memory at all for the dates or times of events discussed.

18. Riley D. and Shaw M. (1985) *Parental Supervision and the Police*, HORS 83, London, HMSO.

19. Maung N. (1995) *Young People, Victimisation and the Police*, HORS 140, London, HMSO.

20. See Blauner R. (1966) 'Death and Social Structure', *Psychiatry* 29, at 381.

21. But not, it should be noted, in the case of Chris Wilson and his sister, children of Mr and Mrs Wilson. They were not interested in blaming individuals but in tracing the flaws in the system that had been responsible for the release of Jason Mitchell.

22. Drabeck T. and Quarantelli E. (1970) 'Scapegoats, villains and disasters', in J. Short (ed.) *Modern Criminals*, Aldine Press, at 161.

23. See Calasso R. (1994) *The Marriage of Cadmus and Harmony*, Vintage.

24. See Jung C. (1940) *The Integration of the Personality*, Kegan, Paul, Trench, Trubner and Co, esp. at 20.

25. See Littlewood J. 'The denial of death and rites of passage in contemporary societies', in D. Clark (ed.) op. cit., at 69.

26. See Walter T. (1994) *The Revival of Death*, Routledge, at 9.

27. See Murray Parkes C. (1972) *Bereavement: Studies of Grief in Adult Life*, Tavistock, at 8.

28. Blom-Cooper L. (1993) 'Public Inquiries', in M. Freeman and B. Hepple (eds) *Current Legal Problems* 46, Part 2, Oxford University Press at 205.

29. They can be traumatised by murder too, undergoing many of the experiences which I have described: disbelief, confusion, *anomie*, stigmatisation and ostracism. Aftermath, a self-help group founded to support the families of serious offenders, calls its members 'the other victims of crime'.

30. See Christie N. (1977) 'Conflicts as property', *British Journal of Criminology* 17, 1-15.

9

Structural Problems, Perspectives and Solutions

David Carson

Official inquiries into homicides committed by mentally disordered people are biased, or skewed, in favour of certain conclusions and recommendations and against others. Inquiry reports are dominated by descriptions of the conduct of individuals and assessments of their responsibility. Structural factors, an expression which here includes organisational, managerial, policy and procedural matters, receive less attention than they deserve. The objection is not to investigating what the individuals who were involved did, or did not do. Some individuals may deserve criticism. Human behaviour *may* be one of the easiest elements, of the total picture, to change. Recommendations about how individuals should behave in the future may be valuable, even though it will often be difficult to generalise the advice from the particular case to the general. A sound case can be developed for reviewing individuals' contributions to, and responsibility for, the fatal outcome. But that analysis must not be allowed to become exclusive of other analyses, other contributions. The objection is not just to the imbalance and unfairness that results.

The critical problem is with the confused, multiple and arguably contradictory roles that these inquiries have come to assume. Inquiries are not just investigations into, and assessments of responsibility for, what happened. They have acquired cultural and political roles. They are used to focus and to channel disputes, to keep them within manageable proportions, and then to culminate and terminate any controversy with a report.

Once an inquiry has been announced those not involved can sit back, disengage, stop worrying and await the report. Once published the report will be sifted for criticisms that can quickly and easily be explained, for example criticism of levels of resources, or of named individuals. (Some individuals may have to resign even though a comparable level of criticism would not lead to demands for heads to roll in other areas of medicine.) Points which are more difficult to specify, to summarise or to dramatise, which will regularly include structural factors, will tend to be ignored. Then, provided (as is invariably the case) a brief period of potential criticism of the report can be ridden, the report will be treated as ending the controversy. It will no longer be newsworthy. The pressure for change will be off. Only occasionally will the case be kept in the public eye, such as when a newspaper or television programme feels that it can link the issues to other items in the news and retain reader or viewer interest. This occurred with the Ritchie Report on the killing of Jonathan Zito, where particular features, such as the determination of the victim's widow and her generalisation of the issues to include other related cases, have struggled to keep the debate alive.[1]

In these ways 'Inquiries after Homicide' have created a structural imbalance of their own. We ought to be much more critical of these inquiries and suspicious of the roles they play in placating our concerns about the provision of health and community care services for people with mental disorders.

Establishing an inquiry

'Irrationalities' are built into these Inquiries right from the start. They are to be established, the NHS Executive Guidelines advise, when a mentally disordered client kills another person.[2] The determining event is the consequence, a death. That the relatives of the deceased, indeed everyone who despises violence, should wish for some form of an explanation of an untimely death is perfectly understandable. It should be provided. There are a range of fora, including inquests. But using the consequence as the determining factor, as the trigger for establishing inquiries, is inappropriate if the principal objectives, or even just key objects (as explicitly stated in paragraph 33 of the circular), are to learn from the past with a view to preventing recurrence.

Death is the manifestation of a possible problem. But it is not the problem itself. The problem is that danger *may* have been poorly predicted and/or badly managed. The death may suggest, but it does not prove, that there is a problem. Is it not obvious that we should not have to wait for a death to occur before we become anxious that danger may be being poorly predicted and/or managed? Focusing on the outcome rather than the problem is, at the very least, inappropriate and inefficient. Responding with inquiries into the outcome of death, rather than the problem of possibly poor process control, distracts our attention away from the key issues.

The death may have occurred because, in the particular facts of the case, emergency medical services were not available soon enough to save the victim. If the victim is saved there is no requirement of an inquiry. If the victim is not saved then there must be an inquiry. Why not inquire into near deaths, into serious injuries, into attempted murders? They will often be more deserving of understanding and learning, not least because they are more common. Such inquiries are permitted, but not required.

If the goals are, or even just include, learning and prevention then the focus needs to be the assessment and management of danger, whatever the actual outcome. Good fortune may have prevented a death from occurring. For that we may and should be grateful. But as good fortune is not predictable it cannot be, and should not be, relied upon for coming to the rescue. Good fortune is not a management tool. There is, potentially, as much to be learnt from a near homicide as from the real thing. Death is, it is submitted, being improperly used as a convenient demarcation line for deciding when to hold a full inquiry. It is particularly surprising that this rule has been propagated by a public authority which is concerned about the quality of management skills and practices.

However, full inquiries cannot be held into every actual or potentially dangerous incident involving mentally disordered people. There would be too many. It is not just a question of the expense of inquiries (time as well as fees), but many other issues including the ability of organisations to assimilate and learn from so many different messages. Indeed, it is submitted that there are already too many inquiries into homicides for organisations to cope with. The argument here is not for more inquiries. It is for an appropriate test or rule for deciding when inquiries should be established. Such a rule should be related to the objectives of, and potential benefits realisable from, inquiries. Unfortunately, at the moment, the role of inquiries in appeasing controversy dominates over learning and prevention goals.

There is a hierarchy of inquiries. A judicial inquiry appears to be universally regarded as *la crème de la crème*. Public inquiries are preferred over private. A lawyer chair appears to be regarded as essential if the inquiry is to have any gravitas. The more inquiry members, then the more powerful or persuasive the conclusions and recommendations, appears to be the assumption. A dedicated secretariat demonstrates serious intentions.

A homicide by someone without a mental disorder rarely merits any kind of inquiry other than a trial. Shamefully reinforcing the unfounded stereotypes of 'dangerous madmen', the rules provide that a mentally disordered person killing another person automatically leads to a full independent inquiry, on top of the trial. However a mentally disordered person killing himself or herself only merits a multi-disciplinary inquiry.[3]

It is not just a case of demeaning the value of the lives of people with mental disorders. The mere requirement, in cases of suicide, of a local multi-disciplinary audit does not make sense if the object is to learn from and to prevent recurrences. First, a mentally disordered person killing himself or herself, let alone attempting to do so, is a *much* more likely occurrence than a mentally disordered person killing another. If independent inquiries, especially those with all the trappings, are more insightful and valuable than other kinds of inquiry, then why are they not involved where the deaths are much more common, where more lives are being lost? Secondly, how a suicide was able to occur, when someone was known to be mentally disordered and distressed, is liable to be as difficult, if not more difficult, a question to answer. For example, with a suicide the perpetrator cannot be questioned.

If 'Inquiries after Homicide' were designed to help everyone to learn what happened and to help reduce the likelihood of recurrence, then they were badly designed. As birds they are kiwis. If the object is to understand and learn then we should establish appropriate instruments. Unfortunately the learning and preventing goals have been subverted.

Hindsight

Ostensibly an inquiry is established in order to discover what, if anything, 'went wrong' and to learn lessons for the future. Given that mental health services necessarily involve taking risks – for example, our legislation requires the interests of patients and public to be balanced – it ought to be possible for an inquiry to report that 'nothing went wrong' although the harm that occurred is regrettable. But can we expect an inquiry ever to come to such a conclusion? Would we not, as consumers of inquiry reports, be very disappointed with such a conclusion and feel that we had been cheated of our criticisms? Popular reasoning, which the automatic establishment of an 'Inquiry after Homicide' reinforces, has it that since harm resulted there must be someone to criticise. As Dowie observed:

> *To assume that a bad outcome implies a bad decision is the most fundamental and widespread of all fallacies!* (emphasis in original.)[4]

There is an expectation that inquiries will uncover wrongdoing and make criticisms.

However much inquiries may declare that it is unfair and inappropriate for them to luxuriate in the benefits of hindsight, they necessarily do so. They are about blaming, not just learning. Actions by care providers which, alongside hundreds and thousands of similar decisions each day and week, were taken rapidly and as part of systems or processes, are individually abstracted, described, mulled over and commented upon in detail, all with the benefit of hindsight.

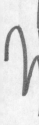

Inquiry reports regularly make interesting, indeed entertaining, reading. The detail they produce is often fascinating. They regularly go back to the perpetrator's childhood, to a lesser extent the victim's, and trace his or her history. Perhaps we, as readers, wish someone would pay as much attention to our lives, would make our lives famous and significant. We forget, while we read these details, that they are, basically, insignificant. The only thing that makes them interesting, indeed the only reason a report was written about them, is what happened later: the homicide. As readers, just like the inquiry team, we are caught up in hindsight. Were it not for the death we would not be reading it, it would not have been written, it would not be interesting. Death makes it fascinating.

As readers of novels we know that authors have to be selective, that they will highlight certain events, that they will skip over the mundane. But these reports are not novels and they should neither be written nor read as such. Nevertheless little attention is paid, in the writing of inquiry reports, to explaining the rules of inclusion and exclusion. The reader takes on trust (for he or she has no option) the writers' decisions about what is worthy and unworthy of inclusion. Should the reader's trust be so readily bestowed? For example, what about the incidents that are not described? Is that because they were irrelevant, and if so why? Is it because there is no evidence, or no reliable evidence, about them? If so, have sufficient steps been taken to obtain that evidence given that it might lead to different conclusions? Or was it excluded for some other reason? Are we always told?

The story-telling model, so automatically expected of inquiries and so readily adopted by them, may be very inappropriate, indeed dangerously deceptive. Where should an inquiry's inquiry begin and end? The death, and the response to it, provides one dimension. But the choice of 'the other end' can effectively determine the whole thrust of the report's conclusions and assumptions. The detailed history of events becomes a challenge that has to be mastered. Having done so both the inquiry members and we, as their readers, naturally feel that that detail must be significant. But descriptions of events may be seductive. It is so much easier to describe an act or behaviour than it is, for example, to convey the significance or intensity of a system of thought, expectations, patterns of behaviour, or how difficult it is, in practice, to stop and think of alternative procedures or explanations.

Inquiries come to conclusions. In doing so they implicitly adopt explanatory theories. But they do not, explicitly, test theories. Different possible explanations, both for individual incidents and to summarise sequences of events, are offered by different witnesses and any counsel to the inquiry. But there is no direct parallel with the scientific model of testing hypotheses. The inquiry's report will be written in a style and with an air of being 'the answer'. The contested incidents have been inquired into and the inquiry team reveals 'the truth' about them. In this inquiry reports mirror court judgements and pronouncements. Indeed, the similarity to judicial decisions may provide inquiry reports with additional prestige.

Most of our court proceedings, however, are adversarial: the court has to choose between the two invariably competing sides – prosecution or defence, plaintiff or defendant. The court relies upon the parties developing their theories about the disputed events. It only has to choose between them. In doing so the court regularly relies upon rules concerning which side has the job of proving their case and the extent to which they must do so: the onus and burden of proof. Thus, we never hear judges or courts declare, directly or in effect: 'I am sorry but I just cannot be sure about this.'

Courts always make decisions (although there may be delays), because the rules about who must prove and to what degree are there to help them out when in doubt. Inquiries, however, are much more investigatory. The inquiry members, and/or their counsel, develop their own theories and consider those of the different witnesses. They are not bound by rules about who must prove what and to which degree of reliability. This is an advantage because the inquiry is not limited to just two competing overall theories. But it also emphasises that we should never read or treat inquiry reports in the same way as court decisions. We do not know, and inquiry reports tend not to tell us, to what level of proof the different findings of fact have been made. We know what the report tells us; we do not know

what other explanations have been considered and rejected. We are rarely told which conclusions the inquiry members are uncertain about. Although entirely different procedures are involved, we are as unlikely to hear an inquiry report that it cannot be sure what happened as we are to hear such an admission in a court.

Strictly inquiry reports are, in reality, just one more theory about what happened. However, because of the processes that inquiries adopt, their theories are more deserving of respect than many, if not all, others. Those theories are both as strong and as weak as the processes the inquiry adopted. But theory it remains. A little more modesty or diffidence about the conclusions might be merited, or more rigorous explanations of or justifications for those conclusions. Court decisions on a specific issue (e.g. guilt or blame for pre-stated allegations) can be appealed; inquiries' conclusions on a wide range of issues and events cannot.

Facts

Inquiries are, we seem to believe, very skilful at discovering what happened. But are they? The detail and the story-line give a powerful impression of veracity. But they are necessarily partial descriptions of 'external' events: who did what to whom, when, to what effect. Much less attention is paid to the 'inner' events, how people interpret, understand, rationalise, etc., their activities. Both are essential for an understanding of what happened. That a clinician prescribed a particular drug tells us about external acts. It tells us nothing about his or her decision-making processes, let alone how he or she perceives and values the many difficult issues of principle involved.

Try it this way. Imagine that you are a skilful actor. You have read an inquiry report. You now have to act the part of one of the principal people involved in a re-enactment. The report will provide you with plenty of stage directions about what you are to do and where. But does it provide you with sufficient information in order to 'get under the skin' of your character? Without getting into theories of acting, do you understand the motivation of your character? You know what your character did, if we assume that the outward acts have been accurately described, but do you understand why he or she behaved that way? Could you accurately *ad lib* for your character? You may know the decisions that your character took, for example a decision to discharge a patient from hospital, but could you articulate your character's reasons for that decision?

Try it another way. Think about what you have done over the past two weeks. Now imagine those activities as described in an inquiry report. Do you think that that description provides a sufficient and an accurate description of your last two weeks? Our behaviour is the product of a rich variety of factors, only some of which we can describe and understand. Our behaviour, as also our thinking, is largely patterned. We make assumptions about the world and other people in it. We are guided by values and assumptions, many of which are inexplicit. For example, mental health workers have views about the rightness and appropriateness of imposing treatment, let alone particular treatments with disturbing side-effects. They have different views about how important it is to regard patients as responsible for their own behaviour. They have similar but different experiences and goals. This richness, which reflects real life, tends to be absent from inquiry reports.

But, some would argue, that does not matter. Inquiries are supposed to find out what happened, that is who did what, and then go on, where appropriate, to allocate blame. That only requires finding and describing the 'outer facts'. But, even if that were a truthful statement of the goals of inquiries, it is inappropriate. Blame cannot be fairly attached without an understanding of the reasons and motivations for behaviour. It is one thing to make a driver strictly liable, so that his or her reasons and excuses become irrelevant, for parking on a double yellow line. It is entirely different to blame, for example, a psychiatrist for discharging a patient who went on to kill another person just on the basis of the 'outer facts' about the decision. A much wider range of information, such as the service's goals, philosophy and values, experiences, policies and procedures, needs to be taken into account if the decision is to be understood. This is even more important if it is conceded that prevention of recurrence is a goal. If you want to change individuals' behaviour you need to take into account, at the very least, 'why' as well as 'what' issues.

Causation

You are driving your car around a corner when another car collides with you. What happened? Who is responsible? An inquiry will not be established to answer these questions for you. Rather you may have to go to court to gain compensation, or to be a witness when the other driver is charged with some criminal offence, where the courts' decisions will answer your question about responsibility (at different standards of proof between the civil and criminal courts). Or will they?

The courts will decide whether there is sufficient evidence that what the driver did constituted an offence and whether there is sufficient evidence that the driver was negligent. That tells us about blame, or legal responsibility. But that is only part of the picture.

Invariably there are many reasons for, causes of, a car accident. If there were not then why do have research into road safety? Contributing, occasionally principal, reasons include the quality of the road, road surfaces, lighting, tyres, car design, speed limits. But these reasons are rarely important for a court to know about. If there is nobody else to blame then a victim, needing compensation, may decide to sue the agency responsible for the roads. But if we can blame an identifiable individual then we need look no further.

Inquiry reports seem to adopt a similar, legalistic, approach to the issues of causation and responsibility facing them. 'Responsibility' is associated with such concepts as blame, culpability, with moral responsibility. But it can have a much more neutral meaning associated with cause. 'Who is responsible?' can mean 'Who is to be blamed?' or 'Who caused this?' They are different questions. If your objective is to blame people, whether fairly or to scapegoat them, then the first meaning is appropriate. But if your objective is to learn, hopefully to avoid repetition, then the second meaning is appropriate.

Blaming individuals involved with mentally disordered people who killed someone may, sometimes, be appropriate. But that still does not answer the question about responsibility. What were the other, non-trivial, causal factors? We do not tackle road safety problems exclusively by identifying and blaming bad drivers. Initiatives to improve roads, for example clearer hazard signs, or to change 'cultural' aspects of driving, such as by educating drivers about the effects of alcohol or the speeds which can seriously injure or kill children, can have a preventive effect independent of identifying and blaming individuals. The analogy is appropriate. If we wish to learn and to prevent then we need to consider a wide range of possible causes. Action on these other causes may be more productive.

An inquiry report may identify one or more individuals as responsible, say a psychiatrist. Consider the response of psychiatrists working in similar posts but in a different service. If the psychiatrist is criticised, blamed, perhaps held up to ridicule, then other psychiatrists are liable to respond that the report is irrelevant to them. That individual was to blame, was wrong. That is what caused the homicide. 'I', they may say to themselves, 'do not anticipate being similarly negligent, blameworthy. The report has nothing to tell me, other than to reinforce the importance of avoiding negligent practice, about how I do my work.' Thus concentrating upon individuals' contributions, enabling their portrayal as idiosyncratic practitioners, inhibits the effectiveness of any general message about how such incidents may be prevented in the future.

Alternatively the psychiatrist reader, or any other person involved in providing mental health services who reads inquiry reports in order to try to learn from them, may respond with some expression or feeling akin to: 'There but for the grace of God go I.' In such cases the report is likely to have found an individual to have been responsible but not attached much opprobrium to his or her acts. But readers who respond in that way have nothing to learn from. They are attributing the causes of the incident to bad luck. They are demonstrating their belief system, which ought to shock managers, employers and inquiries, that they can be held responsible, and possibly be condemned, for bad luck. They will reason that they can do nothing about bad luck. It is not a management tool. If inquiries wish to have an effect in reducing the need for inquiries, rather than just pinpointing individuals for blame, they ought to consider how their reports might be able to help.

Individuals, organisations and structures

Inquiry reports are so dominated by, and we are so accustomed to, descriptions of the actions of individuals told in story format, that alternative approaches do not seem regularly to be considered. For example, take the findings and comments in 1994 of the Ritchie Inquiry. Arguably its most important and significant comments, particularly with a view to prevention of recurrence, were:

> In the course of our inquiry, it has been noticeable how little routine attention appears to have been paid to [sic] anybody to quality or outcome measurement of the community management of mentally ill people. The same is true of the performance of staff, either as individuals or as teams. There seem to have been no consequences whether the work was done well or done badly. Those who planned procedures or made policies do not appear to have checked or to know whether they were being followed.[5]

This observation is almost a 'by the way' statement. The points were noticed on passing. The Inquiry did not set out to investigate these points. It did not have explicit theories to test either about the existence of monitoring procedures or their significance as causal theories. Indeed the Inquiry Team are careful to write 'appears,' 'seem to' and 'do not appear to', presumably because they failed specifically to test these theories with their witnesses. The comment is almost an afterthought.

Those people responsible for planning procedures, making policies and measuring the effectiveness of outcomes do not figure as characters in the story. It is not just that it is difficult to care, one way or the other, about unnamed characters in a story. It is that the story-telling approach or model effectively writes them out. In a story-telling format it is so much easier, and more readily expected, to describe individuals' acts than to describe, in theory or practice, either monitoring procedures, or the ways in which information flows, or the ways in which both individuals and the system learn.

The Inquiry into Andrew Robinson's killing of Georgina Robinson provided a very detailed history of Andrew Robinson's involvement with mental health care services.[6] The Inquiry members conclude in their preface that the service managers and practitioners could, and should, have avoided many of the deficiencies that their Report reveals.[7] The Inquiry Team continue:

> it is, however, our view that much of the maladministration and malpractices derived from a fundamentally flawed statutory framework.[8]

They devote a chapter to arguing for a very different statutory framework. In doing so they echo arguments which had been developed by the Mental Health Act Commission, of which two members of the inquiry had been Chair and Vice-Chair.

There may be a compelling case for radical statutory reform. An inquiry may illustrate the case, but that was not, at least directly, how the argument was developed in this Report. Indeed the detail for the proposed new statutory framework is singularly lacking. The Report concentrates upon what individuals did, and did not, do. The Inquiry Team specifically looked at the design and related features of the unit where the death took place. However, the Report does not focus upon management practices in any very direct fashion or detail. 'Management' is treated as an amorphous corporate entity not made up of individuals with roles, duties and responsibilities in any manner comparable to clinicians. For example, in a chapter which must, given its centrality to mental health care practice, be regarded as critical, it considers risk assessment and management. It states that 'these concepts are new to psychiatry', which may surprise many, especially forensic psychiatrists.[9] It calls for regular risk assessments and risk management but, admittedly like other reports on this topic, presumes first, that everyone knows what risk assessment involves and, secondly, treats it as exclusively a responsibility of the individual practitioners. That involves a dangerously narrow conception of risk and its potential for management.[10] In fairness to the Inquiry, it is notable that they requested that a seminar be organised for them on risk assessment and management, whose proceedings were published at the same time as the Report in a companion volume.[11] However, the Report does not develop those ideas into, for example, a statement of managers' duties in risk assessment or principles of good practice.

Inquiring into the problem, e.g. managing danger

The Report of the Inquiry into the case of Andrew Robinson notes, in respect of risk management, that:

> The availability of information at the right time is crucial, and there is a major administrative task in ensuring that systems are in place which are failsafe against human forgetfulness and work overload.[12]

But where, in the analysis of what happened in the particular case, is this need illustrated? Where, in the argument for a radically different statutory structure, are the implications of this point made? Inquiry reports tend to make general points or sweeping assertions on managerial issues. They rarely get entangled in management perspectives or assessments of managers' direct responsibilities. There are plenty of management texts on good practice concerning information and decision-making. Why do not inquiries call expert witnesses on system design, monitoring, information processing, service planning and judge individual managers by those criteria? It would be fairer to managers to treat them as individuals and judge them against contemporary professional standards.

Risk decisions, for example about whether a mentally disordered patient is safe enough at a particular time, place and activity, may be made by practitioners. Those decisions may be the obvious starting place for an assessment of the quality of risk assessment and management. But others have their contributions. The resource context is critical. A risk can be made much safer, for example, by increasing the level of supervision or monitoring. That depends upon the resources available, which will often not be within the control of the decision-makers. Resources will be finite and someone will be making decisions about how they can be invested to maximum advantage. Inquiries could, and should, undertake an analysis of the efficiency of the investment of the resources available to a service. Are individual decision-makers, such as clinicians, supported by planners and managers in order to ensure the most efficient use of resources? Can clinicians quickly call upon resources to help manage a risk?

Risk-taking does, indeed, depend upon the quality of the information available to the decision-maker. It also depends upon its relevance and reliability. The focus ought to be on the purpose rather than the means, that is on the decision rather than just the information available. Information may be interesting but that does not, necessarily, make it relevant. Different kinds of information will be needed for different kinds of risk. Different people will hold different information for different purposes. Management systems are needed to ensure that relevant information is being collated, tested for accuracy and relevance, and is available when and where needed. Inquiries could conduct audits of the information that is available for different mental health service purposes, its accuracy, relevance and speed of availability.[13]

The focus should be on decision-making rather than just information. Decision-making requires the exercise of judgment on many issues, including the amount of time and information that are necessary for taking the decision. Decision-making is a discrete subject, or science.[14] Decision-makers can be trained; better decisions can be made. Indeed, a decision-making focus is critical because of the many ways in which individuals can, quite innocently, make errors of different kinds arising out of the difficulties we have, as humans, with managing information. One of the most common sources of error involves the undervaluing of base-rates. We tend to underestimate the significance of the background information that applies to all cases, for example age, and to overestimate the significance of unique information about the particular case. We also tend to overestimate the likelihood of outcomes that are regarded as dramatic. For example the likelihood of a person with a mental disorder committing suicide is regularly, and dramatically, underestimated in comparison with the likelihood of homicide by a person with a mental disorder. (Automatic homicide inquiries reinforce this misperception.)

We also regularly overestimate our abilities to manipulate information. Consider, for example, that it is often suggested we are only capable of manipulating seven pieces of information at a time. If that is the case then consider what happens in risk assessment. Take just one piece of information, such as concern about future violence by a patient, based upon his past violence: (1) There is the degree of harm to consider, how much. (2) There is the length of time that the patient or others will be at risk, how long. (3) There is the likelihood of furure violence. (4), (5) and (6) There is the reliability of each of those assessments. (7) The information collected has to be considered in the context of the risk decision that is being proposed. Now how about considering a second piece of information?

Inquiries could require employers to produce any decision aids with which they supply their staff. They could examine the continuing education and training programmes in decision-making (particularly risk assessment and management) which the employers provide. They could examine the thoroughness of any learning loops established to ensure that both the individuals and the organisation learn from decision-making.

It is a management responsibility to ensure that staff are competent and keep up-to-date with developments. It is their responsibility to train, supervise and support their staff in decision-making. The specialist knowledge and research skills necessary to investigate and assess risk factors have to remain with particular disciplines, such as psychiatry, psychology and social work, but the management of that information is a separate matter. That is a responsibility of managers and employers. The integration and management of information from several different disciplines, particularly when it crosses organisational boundaries (such as between health and social services, hospitals and community) is 'out of the hands of' the practitioner disciplines. It is very much a management issue.

Unfortunately inquiries concentrate upon the relatively 'easy-to-see' contributions and responsibilities of individuals and tend to overlook the critical role of managerial support and guidance. Inquiries could inquire into 'the risk-taking success rates' that managers monitor, if they do. This would include obtaining a ratio of 'correct' assessments of safety to 'incorrect' assessments, not just the errors. Admittedly there are many problems in collecting and defining such data, for example the success or failure may not have been due to the decision, but consider the implications of an organisation not actively seeking that kind of information. It does not know what is going on, how successful it is being, whether it is getting better.

Although inquiries are only established where danger may have been under-predicted and someone has died, the research repeatedly demonstrates that dangerousness is over-predicted.[15] There appears to be some form of consensus about the current ratio of true to false positive assessments of dangerousness. Any public protest or pressure seems to be towards encouraging more false positive assessments, although that is not authorised by the law. But what should that ratio, between true and false predictions of danger, be? Who should be determining and reviewing it? Inquiries seem to see such issues as exclusively the concern of clinicians. The Mental Health Act 1983 requires a balancing of public safety and patients' rights. While we do not hold automatic inquiries into false positive assessments of danger (even though they are much more common), clinicians know that their decisions to detain may be challenged before, and reversed by, Mental Health Review Tribunals. But hospital managers also have responsibilities for reviewing the detention of patients. Should not the policies, assumptions, practices, objectives and values that are implicit in the balancing decisions about dangerousness be made explicit, insofar as they can be explicit? Should not employing authorities and managers 'own', and be publicly responsible for, the criteria and procedures adopted when decisions involving patients' civil liberties and public safety are made?

Mental health care is, quite rightly, a very controversial subject. Service providers necessarily work within a special statutory framework which provides some guidance for making decisions about the delicately balanced issues. But it provides remarkably limited guidance. Do inquiry reports, which have the authority to praise and condemn, provide more useful information on such topics? It is submitted that they do not. They certainly provide more detailed lists of things that can go wrong, of things to be avoided, of the horrors that await certain practitioners. But guidance about how patients' rights are to be balanced with public safety is singularly lacking. The 'hot potato' is, conveniently, left with the individuals who have to take the decisions.

The Ritchie Report noted:

> We are very concerned that these failures may well be reproduced all over the country, in particular in poor inner city areas. We have heard time and again throughout the Inquiry, that Christopher Clunis is not alone, that there are many more like him living in the community who are a risk to themselves or to others.[16]

An acid question: Do inquiry reports make it easier to identify these other Christopher Clunis people? Perhaps one inquiry report should adopt the thesis that it is possible to show how such cases could and should be identified and acted upon.

Providing quality mental health services necessarily involves having 'errors'. For example, take an interim secure unit which has to decide whether patients, who are detained there because they are perceived to be dangerous, are to be allowed temporary leave from the unit. A patient may not return at the agreed time, or may behave inappropriately when away from the unit. That unit may appear to have 'perfect' results. There may be no cases where temporary leave is abused. Does it follow that it has perfect decision-making? No. The best way to ensure that temporary leave is not misused is not to grant it. The unit's success may be entirely due to having a very conservative risk-taking practice. If we only look at the false negatives, the people wrongly assessed as not being dangerous, we get a very partial picture. The quality of the decision-making can only be judged if we also know about the false positive assessments. If a service is not making any false negative decisions then that is very likely to be due to making a high ratio of false positive decisions. In practice services need to make some false negative decisions in order to know that they are somewhere near 'the balance point'. It is to be hoped that those will be decisions where skilful risk management devices have been devised in order to reduce the consequences of 'failure'.

Blaming managers and employers

If managers tend to 'get off lightly' from inquiry reports, those above them, responsible for the design of the frameworks, the policies and the systems that managers have to implement, invariably escape close scrutiny. Certainly inquiry reports are quickly read to see if there is a criticism of government, particularly for under-resourcing services. But that should not be the limit of the inquiry. How could the Inquiry into the case of Andrew Robinson emphasise that much of the 'maladministration' was the consequence of an inappropriate statutory framework without going on to demonstrate and to blame government for its failure to monitor the consequences of its laws and policies?[17] If the statutory framework is causing or contributing to problems then action by government is as desirable as if an individual's behaviour had been criticised. Arguably, it is more important because the statutory structure is more general and affects many more cases than does the individual's contribution. But such comments in reports, largely because they are not attached to an individual's name, lack censure, although it is notable that the Woodley Team Report tried hard in its criticism of the Government's legislative response, the *Mental Health (Patients in the Community) Bill*, describing it as 'seriously flawed'.[18]

The House of Commons Select Committee, involving elected representatives with special interests in health, is in a powerful position but avoids the issues; for example they declare, when considering the care of seriously mentally ill people, that

> the safety of the public must be the paramount consideration in Government policy-making on this issue.[19]

But that contravenes the *Mental Health Act 1983*, enacted by the House of Commons, which requires decision-makers also to take other considerations into account.

A common theme of inquiry reports concerns breakdowns or

deficiencies in communication. Individuals may have fallen down on the job and deserve criticism. But their job may have been made very much more difficult by the structures within which they had to carry out their jobs. The organisational divide between health and social services cannot make communication easier, although there may be countervailing justifications for it. Health and social services authorities who do not have co-terminous boundaries have problems structured into them.

Team-work is regularly lauded. But if it is so important then why is not made easier by ensuring that management structures work for, rather than against, practitioners? For example, many practitioners find it useful to make 'contracts' with their patients or clients. This demonstrates and reinforces the reciprocal nature of therapy and emphasises the patient's or client's contribution to mental health. But these 'contracts' are not legally binding. Why are not legal and other structures devised to assist service delivery? The finding that the law frequently produces counter-therapeutic effects has led to a major movement in the United States, known as therapeutic jurisprudence, to show how law reform could assist.[20]

It may never be possible to draw a direct causal link between a homicide and a fault in the way that managers have designed and monitored services. However, as the Woodley Team Report noted:

> the lack of separation of assessment and care management from service providers in psychiatric services is, in our view, a critical constraining factor in tailoring services to meet individual needs.[21]

Managers may escape that sort of blame. But that is only one way of looking at causation. If inquiries were more realistic and spent more time looking at the volume of work and the number of risk decisions taken around the time of 'the fatal decisions', then they might be able to assess how valuable a different system of work might have proved. Different ways of working might have 'freed up' time and other resources so permitting more attention to be paid to the problematic working practices. For example, there are communication problems when discharge letters, from hospitals to general practitioners, are de-layed. Consultants have limited time. They may have to sign these letters, be responsible for them. Much time might be saved, however, by allowing nurses to draft the letters. Develop-ing a job-description for 'information managers', to ensure that reliable, accurate and relevant information is available when and where needed, and to ensure the collection and pres-entation of feedback to assist learning, may have much more to offer than debating the criteria for inclusion upon registers.

It would not, it is submitted, be too inappropriate a reading of recent inquiry reports to generalise them as condemning the system but criticising individuals. To the extent that that is a fair reading it distracts attention and dissipates efforts. It is only too easy to reason that since the problems in that other service were due to 'rogue practice' the inquiry report has little to offer local services. Too little attention is paid to the contribu-tions of individual practitioners with relatively little effect upon managers, employers and those with control over the design, planning and resourcing of services. Take the Woodley Report, for example.[22] In a section headed 'Overview', where S.L. is the mentally disordered person living in the community who kills someone in a social services day centre, they conclude:

> Our main criticism over the period of S.L.'s care and treatment in the community is that attempts to provide him with good social care were undermined by inadequate health care....
> We have identified the following contributory factors which militated against high quality care in the community by both health and social services:
> * organisational change
> * pressures on human resources
> * poor communications
> * poor administrative systems
> * lack of effective risk management
> * lack of effective multi-disciplinary working
> * inexperience.

With those 'contributory factors' is it surprising that there was inadequate health care? Which causes which? Is it more likely that the poor health care caused the seven contributory prob-lems identified or that the seven problems, which are all the responsibility of managers, caused or contributed to the poor health care? Is it realistic to expect adequate health care, let alone high quality health care, to be provided when there are such organisational and administrative problems? Are individual practitioners' contributions to be expected to surmount such a collection of managerial problems? Why are the contributions of individual service providers, but not managers and employers, isolated?

Lawyers in the chair

Under the NHS Guidelines, health and local authorities are encouraged to appoint a lawyer to chair inquiries into homicides.[23] They are thought to bring special skills to the task. But is this the case? They are, generally, more likely to ensure that important procedural considerations, such as the principles of natural justice, are adhered to. But those objectives might be achieved by having a lawyer available to give advice on such issues, as occurs in magistrates' courts with justices' clerks or in courts martial. Most of the points could also be met by clear procedural guidance notes.

Lawyers are considered skilful in finding, sifting and assessing facts. But is this because they are good at the task or just because they are associated with it? A major problem with lawyers is their lack of scientific orientation. They are very good, persuasive, at asserting causes and effects. But they are very poor at checking the reliability of their inferences. Certainly we have to act upon a judge's decision; but it does not follow that it was correctly made. We ought to be very suspicious of the process whereby the outcome of a trial may be hotly debated, the decision may be considered finely balanced, but when the court renders its judgement all that debate quickly dissipates. Whether witnesses are more willing to reveal information in private hearings than in public inquiries might be investigated empirically. Why are debates about legal processes so often conducted just in terms of assertion and counter-assertion? Cross-examination is regularly held up as an exceptional tool for discovering liars. But is it? Individual witnesses may have changed their evidence during cross-examination. But it does

142   *David Carson*

not follow that the first statements were lies and the second the truth! It may be dramatic but it does not follow that cross-examination is a tool for truth-finding.[24] Confessions, whether in police stations or in courtrooms, are unreliable evidence. Lawyers declare that their techniques are effective, invariably based upon anecdotal evidence, but rarely put them to the test. Lawyers are very good at challenging each other, standing up for their clients, criticising and appealing against judges' decisions. But they are very poor at investing in research into their own basic techniques, challenging cherished assumptions.

Many of the criticisms levelled at inquiries that were detailed above, such as focusing on identifiable individuals and narrow conceptions of cause and responsibility, arise from the approaches that lawyers tend to adopt in their practices. Even if appropriate in adversarial trials, they are damaging in inquiries where one object is to learn for the future. However, simply not having lawyers to chair the inquiries would be an inadequate response. There are too many assumptions, too many expectations, about how inquiries ought to operate to overcome with just such a change. An overhaul of how we view the problems and the best ways of learning is necessary.

It needs to be appreciated that courts, and similar judicial bodies, are also making risk decisions. There is a risk, even with provision for multiple appeals, that the courts get it wrong, convict or compensate the wrong person. They may call it making judgements, rather than 'risk-taking', but it remains, analytically, a risk decision. Despite recent concern about mistaken convictions (and note that concern has been with regard to high profile cases where considerable sums have been invested in assuring the quality of the proceedings), the Royal Commission on Criminal Justice did not adopt an analysis which focused on the quality of the decision-making process.[25] Should not lawyers demonstrate that they are active in reducing the risk of wrongful decisions by courts and tribunals before they judge other disciplines' efforts? Should they not demonstrate competence in risk research and risk management in their own fields of operation before they comment on the practices of others? Inquiries chaired by people skilled in system design or competent to examine structures, processes and practices from a variety of perspectives would be a start.

The moral responsibilities of inquiries

Inquiries are given enormous privileges. They are given extensive moral *authority* to condemn others, with very little right of reply. They have extensive powers over the collection and presentation of information, extensive discretion about how they undertake their work. We ought to consider the moral *responsibilities* of inquiries. A far from complete list of such responsibilities would include, it is submitted, the following.

1. If the homicide was the consequence of bad practice then the inquiry should so declare. But inquiries should be able to convince their readers that had there been no relevant blameworthy conduct they would have so pronounced.

2. While considering 'responsibility' for the homicide, inquiry teams should not limit themselves to any direct precipitating acts by individuals. They should also demonstrate that they have vigorously considered, and fairly assessed the significance of, structural factors.

3. Inquiries should make it plain to their readers what the public legitimately can and cannot expect from mental health care services. They should be explicit about the legislative restrictions on clinicians, including the fact that public safety is not the exclusive criterion for decision-making. They should emphasise that community care, particularly where there are no grounds for detention, is not just a policy but a legal duty. They should be explicit in emphasising that mental health services cannot be provided on a no-risk basis. They should keep repeating what we know about homicides by people with mental disorders, in particular that the risk of violence to others is grossly exaggerated and that it is the apparent randomness in choice of victim, in several cases, that causes much of the public fear.

4. Inquiries, having moral authority, should not avoid the difficult issues. These include such issues as how decision-makers should balance the rights of patients and the public.

They should use their moral authority to help articulate such issues, as a minimum to inform and to encourage debate.

5. Inquiries should explain and justify themselves. They should not just declare their conclusions and make their judgements. For example, they should explain why alternative theories or explanations have been rejected. They should acknowledge when evidence is missing or incomplete. They should explain how sure they are of their own conclusions.

6. Inquiries should explain, clearly, how the services could have been better provided. This should be sufficiently detailed so that readers can understand which decisions and practices should have been different, which were unjustifiable. They should demonstrate that they are making recommendations that are both practical and generalisable.

7. Inquiries should demonstrate that they have been self-critical.

Conclusion

Inquiries discover things about past cases which cause us disquiet. Given that we know that someone has died we feel reassured that the death might not have been entirely in vain. But we may be deluding ourselves with a procedure that owes more to 'buying-off' immediate criticism and demand for action. We need to be much more critical of inquiries and the roles that they play. We owe as much to future as well as past victims.

Notes

1. Ritchie J.H., Dick D. and Lingham R. (1994) *The Report of the Inquiry into the Care and Treatment of Christopher Clunis*, London, HMSO.

2. See earlier chapters in this book for a discussion of circulars HSG (94) 27 and LASSL(94) 4. Selected sections are reproduced in Appendix A.

3. See Appendix A paras 34-5

4. Dowie J. (1990) 'Clinical decision making: risk is a dangerous word and hubris is a sin', in D. Carson (ed.) *Risk-taking in Mental Disorder: Analyses, Policies and Practical Strategies*, Chichester, SLE.

5. Ritchie *et al.* (1994) op. cit., at para 52.0.1.

6. Blom-Cooper L., Hally H. and Murphy, E. (1995) *The Falling*

Shadow: One Patient's Mental Health Care 1978-1983, London, Duckworth.

7. The word 'deficiencies' is noticeably, perhaps deliberately, vague and does not, at least immediately, indicate whether those people are actually being blamed for the death.

8. Blom-Cooper *et al.* (1995) op. cit., preface.

9. Ibid., at 176.

10. Carson D. (1994) 'Dangerous people: through a broader conception of "risk" and "danger" to better decisions', *Expert Evidence* 3(2), 51-69.

11. Crichton J. (ed.) (1995) *Psychiatric Patient Violence: Risk and Response*, London, Duckworth.

12. Blom-Cooper *et al.* (1995) op. cit., at 181.

13. One inquiry team appears to have failed to notice that hospital-based psychiatrists in a unit with which they were concerned only regularly consulted clinical notes, not the separately maintained nursing notes.

14. For example, see Cooke S. and Slack N. (1991) *Making Management Decisions* (2nd ed.), Hemel Hempstead, Prentice Hall.

15. Gunn J. and Monahan J. (1993) 'Dangerousness', in J. Gunn and P. Taylor (eds) *Forensic Psychiatry: Clinical, Legal and Ethical Issues*, Oxford, Butterworth Heinemann.

16. Ritchie *et al.* (1994) op. cit., at para 42.1.2.

17. Blom-Cooper *et al.* (1995) op. cit.

18. Woodley L., Dixon K., Lindow V., Oyebode O., Sandford T. and Simblet S. (1995) *The Woodley Team Report: Report of the independent review panel to the East London and the City Health Authority and Newham Council, following a homicide in July 1994 by a person suffering with a severe mental illness*, London, East London and the City Health Authority, at 140.

19. House of Commons Select Committee on Health (1994) *Better Off in the Community? The Care of People who are Seriously Mentally Ill*, London, HMSO (HC 102-I), at para 33.

20. For ground-breaking work see generally Wexler D.B. (1990) *Therapeutic Jurisprudence: The Law as a Therapeutic Agent*, Carolina Academic Press, Durham (NC); and Wexler D.B. and Winick B.J. (1991) *Essays in Therapeutic Jurisprudence*, Carolina Academic Press, Durham (NC). For references to more recent work see Wexler D.B. (1995) 'Reflections on the scope of therapeutic jurisprudence', *Psychology, Public Policy and Law* 1(1), 220-36, and other papers in, and cited in, a special collection of that journal. For a discussion of the possible implications for the UK see Carson D. and Wexler D.B. (1994) 'New approaches to mental health law: will the UK follow the US lead, again?', *Journal of Social Welfare and Family Law* 79-96.

21. Woodley Team Report (1995) op. cit., at 104.

22. Ibid., at 99-101

23. See Appendix A, para 36 (ii).

24. See Lloyd-Bostock S. (1988) *Law in Practice: Applications of Psychology to Legal Decision Making and Legal Skills*, Leicester, British Psychological Society; and Bartlett D. and Memon A. (1995) 'Advocacy', in R. Bull and D. Carson (eds) *Handbook of Psychology in Legal Contexts*, Chichester, Wiley.

25. Royal Commission on Criminal Justice (Chair: Viscount Runciman) (1993) *Report*, London, HMSO (Cm 2263).

Towards an Audit of Inquiries: Enquiry not Inquiries

Nigel Eastman

Inquiries into homicides by mentally disordered people are mandatory.[1] In contrast, other psychiatric deaths (from suicide) and other medical or surgical deaths are much more commonly solely the subject of local or national audit. Hence, a wholly different governmental approach is adopted to psychiatric homicides from that which is adopted in relation to far more numerous inadvertent surgical and medical deaths. This is probably driven by different public perceptions both of mental illness compared with other illness and of the nature and acceptability of psychiatric risk compared with surgical or other medical risk. Whereas it is frequently perceived as an acceptable risk to die on an operating table at the hands of a (mentally normal) surgeon, it is apparently never, *prima facie*, an acceptable risk to be killed on the streets by someone whose mental state is far from normal. In the latter case the search for explanation and attribution of culpability does not stop at the perpetrator but automatically goes towards those whom it is assumed not only had a duty to treat but also perhaps even to control the perpetrator. Such 'secondary responsibility' is socially and legally peculiar and its pursuit in relation to mentally disordered homicides can perhaps be explained only by virtue of unusual public and governmental fear of the mad, which must be assuaged or limited by the fiction that such harm to others can almost always be controlled, if only things are done properly.

Inquiries are similar to the homicides into which they enquire. Both are 'events'. By contrast, the delivery of mental health care is a process which is more effectively investigated and improved upon by cycles of audit. An inquiry amounts to 'an investigation of circumstances surrounding a mishap' (roughly paraphrased from the *Concise Oxford Dictionary*). It asks a specific question about a specific event. In so doing it takes a 'snapshot' of the activities of professionals and others who were connected with the event, usually using broadly written terms of reference so as potentially to set its own more specific terms of reference, if only as regards the balance of its enquiry between different issues. It also effectively sets its own standards against which it will effectively judge the behaviour of professional staff. More broadly, it effectively sets its own agenda as regards aims (within its terms of reference) and uses a single method usually to pursue a variety of purposes.[2] By contrast, audit is 'dynamic'. It is ongoing and so sets and modifies its terms of reference in the light of experience, always making clear what are the current standards of audit against which performance will be adjudicated. Its methods are clearly defined according to the maximum achievement of its limited purposes. Finally, while inquiries can choose not fully to extend their investigation to the service context within which individual clinicians or other professionals operated, audit can be, and often is, designed as 'service audit' *per se*.[3]

Before my involvement in the seminar which is reported in this book I could not have written the preceding paragraphs. I began the seminar in a state of unfocused unease about the role of mandatory inquiries into homicides by the mentally disordered. I had not been asked to present a paper but to contribute to the discussion arising out of the other papers which are now also reproduced in this book. By the end of the proceedings my unease had become much more clearly focused and also highly reinforced. I moved from sensing that something was wrong with the use of such inquiries, particularly on a mandatory basis, to a much clearer understanding of what exactly it *was* that was wrong. By drawing on, and developing my thoughts on, the other chapters in this book, I hope to describe and justify my new-found clarity and conviction.

The perception of risk and the political imperative

It is accepted, in all medical practice, that there is an inherent benefit/risk ratio and that risk management is part of clinical practice. No one believes that even the most minor surgery is risk free, particularly if it involves a general anaesthetic. Individual patients accept such risks, after they have been properly explained, and there is no presumption of negligence, or usually even the suspicion of negligence, when the risk is realised as a medical mishap. There is only the perceived *possibility* that there *may* have been a breach of duty of care and this *may* have caused the mishap (within the terms of negligence law) and, sometimes, the person who suffered the mishap *may* request what amounts to a legal inquiry into what happened, specifically in terms of the definitions and standards contained within negligence law. The *Bolam* test sets a proper standard by which clinical practice is adjudged, that is, the standard of *a* (not *the*) responsible body of practitioners operating in that particular type of medical situation.[4] The law also sets a standard of 'material contribution' in relation to causation. Only if these two requirements are satisfied is the medical practitioner held liable or even perceived as culpable.

It is implicitly accepted within negligence law that there is an 'irreducible minimum risk'. Indeed, the *Bolam* test does not necessarily imply that a clinician even has to achieve that irreducible minimum risk in relation to every patient in every type of medical situation. The clinician may also properly be able to demonstrate either or both that his clinical action (in terms of the *Bolam* test) was constrained by the quality or availability of resources, which were determined by management, or/and that the resource context in which he operated made a material contribution to causation, therefore limiting or abolishing causation in relation to his own clinical actions. There is, in that sense, a comprehensive inquiry into the mishap which addresses every possible contributory factor. The surgeon is not judged in clinical isolation but in the context of (for example) the operating theatre within which he/she necessarily practised.

By contrast, psychiatric risk is differently perceived and dealt with publicly. Albeit that there can, of course, still be actions in negligence in relation to psychiatric care, a wholly different approach is adopted to psychiatric mishaps specifically where they involve the death of some other person than the patient. The mandatory inquiry represents this different approach. Unlike other medical mishaps, or even psychiatric mishaps where harm accrues solely to the patient, the response by Government and Health Authorities to a mentally disordered homicide includes a substantial political element. Indeed, the imposition of mandatory inquiries into such homicides itself emphasises the substantially political purpose which drives policy in this area. There is, by implication, the initial presumption that 'something must have gone wrong', or at least 'something may well have gone wrong'. There is not even any 'pre-inquiry' which addresses whether or not there is, *prima facie*, the basis for a full inquiry. The risk was realised in a homicide and so there is effectively a *prima facie* presumption that the risk may not have been properly managed. How different this is from the governmental or public attitude even to the poorly performing surgeon who demonstrably has a significantly higher surgical morbidity or mortality rate than the average. Of course, it might be argued that there is a democratic public right, through Parliament and Government, to set whatever it wishes as the 'acceptable risk level' in relation to any particular type of medical mishap. However, aside from the fact that one might properly point to the irrationality of singling out for special consideration mentally disordered homicides (which in any event are very small in number by contrast with other medical mishaps) it is clear that there has been no rational debate about setting some proper level of risk of mentally disordered homicide. By implication, it seems presumed that no risk can be tolerated.

The latter intolerance is reflected in the use of what amounts to 'single variable investigation', whereby the performance of a clinician(s) is adjudged solely on the variable of 'harm to others', solely on that one occasion when the mishap occurred and also solely in relation to that one patient who 'committed' the mishap. Indeed, this perhaps goes to the heart of the inappropriateness of automatically using inquiries rather than audit. Inquiries, by definition, investigate *a* mishap and are therefore, again by definition, 'single variable' in nature. Even though audit *can* be constructed on the basis of a single variable, much more appropriately and commonly it is defined in a comprehensive fashion. A number of targets are set, usually in the knowledge that some of them are mutually exclusive, and an aspect of the standards laid down by the audit (in advance, so to speak) is the acceptable balance between achievement of varying targets. To illustrate the point in relation to secure mental health care, if a clinical team in a medium secure unit were to be shown to have had no absconding from escorted or unescorted parole for ten years this might be seen by the ill-informed as indicative of a high quality of service, simply on the basis that only one variable was being addressed. However, almost certainly, such a team would have been operating over-restrictive practices, thus increasing the average length of time that patients spent in secure care such that it was performing poorly on any reasonable 'rehabilitation' target. The achievement of one target must imply risks of lower performance against some other(s). Similarly, in broader terms, if it is public policy to pursue the target of community care (in general) then it must be accepted that this can only occur at the expense of a higher risk of homicides by the mentally disordered in the community than would otherwise be the case (if all patients were detained in asylums). There is a further inherent problem specifically concerned with pursuing jointly the targets of public safety and avoidance of unnecessary patient restriction (for example, in hospital). Whereas it is possible to know the number of mentally disordered homicides (indeed they are usually blazoned across the tabloid press) it is not possible to know the number of homicides that would *not* have occurred even if a target of a larger number of patients discharged into the community had been achieved. Hence, it is not possible, specifically when using 'avoidance of homicide in the community' as a service evaluation criterion, properly to measure the countervailing variable called 'excess containment in hospital'.

Some general light is perhaps cast upon the unknowable variable, 'excess containment in hospital', by virtue of the fact that there is substantial evidence that the homicide rate for psychiatric patients is little different, overall, from that for the

general population.[5] Albeit that some studies are beginning to
show a possible slight elevation of the risk of homicide or serious
violence by the mentally disordered,[6] even this evidence is not
of an order that could justify wholesale preventive detention.
Even where there is a known risk of past violent behaviour by a
particular patient (it is recognised that the fact and surrounding
circumstances of past violence is the only potentially valid
predictor of future violence) the prediction of future violence on
their part is a hazardous occupation and there may still be little
justification for 'preventive detention'. Certainly, in terms of
public safety, there would probably be a much greater saving of
life arising out of preventative detention of anyone who was
found to be driving a car with more than 80mg per 100mls of
alcohol in their bloodstream than from locking up anyone diagnosed with a serious mental illness.

There is, essentially, an irreducible minimum risk of homicide by anyone and there seems little justification for choosing
even the seriously mentally ill in general as a focus for preventive detention by comparison with members of the general
population, and particularly by comparison with other 'normal'
people who have shown dangerous behaviour to others. Put
simply, the mandatory inquiry approach to mentally disordered
people amounts to another 'ism', that is, 'mental illnessism' or
'mental patientism'. As with all 'ism's', it tends to arise from
deep seated fear of *l'étranger*, and there is no one as *étrange* to
the general public as the mad.

There is a further, and perhaps more understandable, basis
upon which mental mishap risk-taking is perceived and dealt
with differently from other medical risk-taking. The patient who
takes a surgical risk takes it for himself, the doctor being merely
the instrument of risk-taking. By contrast, psychiatrists are (or,
at least, are perceived as) taking risks where the potential
mishap is not only to the patient (for example, suicide) but also
to members of the public. There is perceived 'proxy risk-taking'.
This perception is emphasised by mental health legislation
which allows doctors to detain patients in hospital so as to
reduce their risk to others. Hence, there is separation between
'risk takers' (the doctors) and 'risk acceptors' (members of the
public). This feels inherently uncomfortable, much more so than

the discomfort that the ordinary patient feels when taking a risk at the hands of a surgeon. It may partly be this sense of lack of control which drives public and media attention towards mentally disordered homicides. Not only is there a *risk* being taken (which is bad enough in itself) but someone else is taking it *on my behalf*. There is 'double jeopardy' in terms of events feeling out of control. Hence, inquiries are designed to suggest that future risk to the public can be reduced or even avoided. If a statement can be made about a past mishap of the type 'if only ...' then the public can feel reassured that the future can be safeguarded. It is usually suggested that the object of the 'if only ...' statement can be eliminated, often partly via removal of the particular risk-taker from the game.

The fantasy that public safety can be ensured by some exact science of 'risk assessment and management' is nicely represented in recent utterances of the current Home Secretary,[7] which indicated his intention to extend the types of convictions which would result in a mandatory life sentence. One of the major bases upon which he justified this policy was that, by contrast with determinate sentences (however long), a mandatory life sentence would ensure that, before a prisoner was released, 'there would be proper assessment of his risk', and 'he would not be released until he was shown not to be a risk to the public' (my paraphrasing). These statements imply an accuracy of risk assessment and a level of risk reduction which cannot be achieved and they are essentially a political fraud.

In the mental health field there are also examples going beyond mandatory inquiries which tend to reinforce to the public the fiction that risk can be avoided or greatly controlled. The construction of largely clinically meaningless tools such as supervision registers[8] and 'aftercare under supervision' (*Mental Health (Patients in the Community) Act 1995*) makes the point.[9] Indeed, insistence on the use of the word 'supervision' in both contexts gives the *appearance* to the public that all is well, because all is being 'supervised'. In practice, of course, patients in the community cannot, to any meaningful degree, be 'supervised'. They are autonomous agents who have occasional contact with professional staff. That cannot amount to 'supervision'. The *Concise Oxford Dictionary* defines 'supervise' as 'to oversee, superintend the execution or performance of (thing) or actions or work of (person)'. That is clearly wholly unachievable in relation to a patient living independently in the community.

In summary terms, largely it does not matter how you die. What matters essentially is the probability of death *per se*. There should be a rational public policy approach to the risk of death caused by the mentally ill which emphasises the objective aspects of it and refuses to pay substantial attention to its subjective and emotive aspects. If the chances of being killed by a drunken driver were shown to be twice that of being killed by a mentally ill person, what would be the sense of constructing public policy on the basis of inherently greater fear of the mentally ill? If you were given the opportunity to take a risk of crossing a road containing red cars where there was half the risk of crossing another road with blue cars would you choose the latter because you had an irrational fear of the colour red?

The narrow pursuit of explanation

Inquiries are charged with finding out *what* happened and, further, with finding out *why* a mishap happened. Given there are other means with which to deal with professional irresponsibility or culpability, in my view inquiries should explicitly pursue 'responsibility' solely in the causal sense rather than also in the culpability sense. Of course, in answering the question 'why did the mishap happen?' attention will naturally focus on things that professionals did. However, specifically addressing culpability for what was done is entirely different from use of what was done as an explanation of what happened. Culpability should properly be the concern of bodies charged with maintaining professional standards (such as the GMC) and of the law (which is partly concerned, even in a civil context, with culpability) and should *not* be the business of inquiries. Even though inquiries may not always *overtly* pursue the purpose of establishing culpability, certainly the use to which they are put often goes towards that purpose. This use can at times look something like a public lynching by the tabloid (and even the broadsheet) press. Culpability can be inferred according to a standard which nowhere near accords with those standards required by professional regulatory bodies or by the civil courts.

There is a clear distinction between failure of process or clinical performance *and* such failure having caused a homicide. Clinicians should be judged not according to whether their actions caused a mishap but, rather, according to whether there was a failure of process or performance against accepted professional standards (albeit that in negligence law there is, beyond the *Bolam* test of breach of duty of care *per se*, an *additional* requirement of causation in order to establish negligence as a whole). An error of judgement, even where it led directly to a mishap, is insufficient in law to establish negligence since it does not amount to a breach of the duty of care. The law therefore properly concentrates upon breach of that duty as the first step and only thereafter looks towards causation. By contrast, there is a tendency for inquiries either to conflate breach and causation or to look first towards whether a clinician's actions contributed to a mishap and only then perhaps to look towards whether there was a breach of the duty of care against accepted professional or legal standards. Indeed, there is little evidence that inquiries consciously and overtly adopt for themselves the appropriate professional and legal standards that would be applied elsewhere. In short, inquiries concentrate on what you would expect them to concentrate upon, the mishap itself and its causation. In so doing, they may inappropriately infer culpability, and do it to a lower standard than should be adopted.

Legal, factual and political causation

Legal causation (within negligence law) is assessed to the standard of 'material contribution', using also the 'but for' criterion and the 'foreseeability' criterion. For there to be legal causation the event must have been foreseeable by the person allegedly having breached their duty of care to the other party. The latter aspect of legal causation clearly focuses the mind when applied to homicides by the mentally ill. Would any of the recent homicides into which there have been inquiries have been adjudged legally 'foreseeable'?

Factual causation, that is, what actually caused the mishap, is, of course, usually highly complex. Also, whereas the law addresses each possible element of causation with reference to strict 'material contribution' and 'but for' criteria, inquiries are less strict. They properly address a multitude of potentially causal factors (albeit sometimes within self-imposed constraints by virtue of not always addressing service standards or management). Indeed, this is one of the major advantages of inquiries in the search for explanation in that they are able to range widely across agencies as they see fit. Perhaps herein lies the one valid justification for treating homicides by the mentally disordered differently from suicides, in that non-caring agencies are potentially involved in a causal way in relation to homicides where they are not usually so in relation to suicides. The Ritchie Inquiry into the Care of Christopher Clunis makes this clear through its references to the actions (or inaction) of the police and of the Crown Prosecution Service.[10]

However, factual causation is rendered peculiar in psychiatric deaths (homicides or suicides) by virtue of the fact that a major (if not perhaps *the*) cause of the death was an individual who was not part of the system of agencies into which the inquiry enquires. Ultimately the 'cause' of a homicide is the perpetrator. Only in a secondary sense can anyone else be seen to have 'caused' the killing, by virtue of not controlling the 'primary' cause of the killing. The point is emphasised by turning back to legal causation in that, so far in this country, there is little evidence that the courts have been prepared to accept that a 'secondary causative agent' of a homicide can be liable in negligence by virtue of the conclusion that the killing by his/her patient was 'foreseeable', and that the clinician owed a duty of care to the victim and was in a position to control the patient so as to avert the homicide. By contrast, it seems much more likely that a perpetrator could be in a position to sue his/her own professional carers if they breached their duty of care and if the patient's subsequent mental deterioration was both attributable to the breach of duty of care and caused the homicide. Indeed, there have been such successful litigants;[11] similarly, Christopher Clunis is currently pursuing an action against the health authority responsible for his care in the community while the family of his victim are unable to do so and have felt obliged to pursue an action against him personally.[12]

Far more important in the context of how inquiry reports are *used* than factual and legal causation is what I would call 'political causation'. This is a highly simplified notion of causation which amounts to pursuit, by another name, of the purpose of public reassurance,[13] and which seems achievable only by reference to a small number of simplified factors being perceived as causal of the mishap, preferably including the actions of a particular person(s) who can then be 'disciplined'. Pursuit of this purpose of public reassurance verges on one of the other purposes that Reder and Duncan identify, that of 'catharsis'. Indeed, the two purposes appear to be confused at times. Clearly, political causation is driven by a political imperative which determines a simplicity of attribution which falls well below that required by the pursuit of either legal or factual causation.

Inquiries should be interested in factual causation and, as I have indicated, they are suited for this purpose, and perhaps *only* this purpose. It is likely that there will be many links in a chain of causation leading up to a homicide and, in one sense, many links will likely satisfy the legal criterion of 'but for'. In other words, if only X had not happened then the chain would have been broken. However, that does not mean that only X was a/the 'material cause' of the mishap. Indeed, it is the failure to understand the latter distinction which tends to go with inappropriate attribution of not only causation but also of culpability to single links in the chain (all professionals representing links).

Returning to factual causation, inquiries are not, however, *ideally* constituted for comprehensive enquiry. Even though they may, as did the Ritchie Report, sometimes address resource levels and conclude that they made a contribution to the mishap, there is a strong tendency to deal more with the actions of individual clinicians and other professionals than with the broader resource or service context within which they necessarily operated. This is perhaps understandable since inquiries are not properly equipped to conduct complete surveys of whole services. Even if they can remark, for example, upon the excessive catchment area of a consultant general psychiatrist[14] they are inherently ill-suited to looking into service levels and operation in a detailed way; these are far better addressed by 'service audit'.[15] There should indeed properly be enquiry into management functions such as information systems, funding, nursing ratios and buildings. Similarly, there should perhaps be investigation of such tools as supervision registers,[16] which represent a managerially imposed instrument which has not been clinically generated or tested and which should therefore be addressed essentially managerially. If a doctor is required to utilise registers (according to the criteria in the DOH guidance) then the contribution of registration or non-registration to causation in a particular case should be addressed to a manager and not to a clinician (assuming the clinician operated the register properly in its own terms). The failure to include a manager on inquiry panels emphasises their narrow clinical bias.[17]

Since the cause of a killing is the killer, it is appropriate to ask whether it is *possible* to assess and manage risk such that failure of proper risk assessment or management can *ever be* a causal factor of a homicide by a mentally ill person? Is it possible to 'predict' a killing or merely to say that there is some significant risk of it at some time, thereby distinguishing between the risk of the act *per se* and the prediction of the timing of the act. Bowden[18] argues cogently that, in one inquiry which is represented in the book *The Falling Shadow*,[19] an over-deterministic approach to prediction of violence was adopted. He criticises the book, both because it adopts a journalistic narrative style and because it scape-goats an individual clinician for failing to predict what the inquiry seems to have decided, or even determined, was an entirely predictable event. Bowden goes further and almost ridicules the authors for believing that they knew better than the patient why he killed the victim. Bowden's request, 'listen to the patient', perhaps emphasises the primacy of the role of the patient in any homicide perpetrated by him/her. In a more subtle vein, Grounds has argued against 'hindsight bias',[20] that is, the distorting of real judgements that would or should reasonably have been made at the time when they are viewed in retrospect. Indeed, Bowden himself makes the same point. The question remains, however, as Bowden implicitly argues, as to whether the contribution of a patient is so important and unknowable that a homicide cannot in *any* circumstances be predicted. This probably goes too far. A patient who, while demonstrably coincidentally suffering from specific violent psychotic phenomena, day by day seriously attacks others on a ward, might reasonably be predicted to continue doing so the next day, assuming that his mental state remains untreated and unchanged. If we conclude that we might reasonably predict further violence and its timing in this case then we have accepted that there is a valid notion of 'prediction' *per se* and all that is at issue is the data that will successfully predict. Bowden's point is perhaps that, in the majority of cases, where the patient is not repeatedly violent, episodes of violence are isolated and are therefore essentially 'unpredictable'. This causes me to return to the distinction between the act *per se* and the timing of the act. Perhaps ultimately that is the important distinction in terms of prediction, and therefore, by implication, in terms of foreseeability and causation.

Methods of investigating factual causation

Are inquiries, as currently constituted, the most efficient means by which to establish the truth of factual causation of a mentally disordered homicide *and* to learn from that knowledge so as to modify services in a cumulative way? I think the answer is no, and I hope that what follows justifies that conclusion.

Efficiency in determining the explanation of a particular mishap

An inquiry becomes a constituent part of the 'catastrophic event' which is represented by its homicide. By contrast, mental health services represent a process, both inherently and over time, and are capable of evolution along a 'learning curve'. One of Reder and Duncan's four purposes,[21] that of 'catharsis', perhaps emphasises the 'event' nature of an inquiry, since it is not possible to have a continuously developing cathartic process which goes on for ever. The political purpose of an inquiry is to 'exorcise' the public grief and fear that arises from a homicide and its consequent political harm. However, it seems inherently unlikely that pursuit of catharsis will necessarily efficiently coincide with elucidation of the truth. Catharsis is an inherently emotional pursuit which has nothing necessarily to do with objectivity or truth. Indeed, the truth of an event may be anything but cathartic and perhaps this partly explains why the media distorts inquiry reports so as to simplify and overemphasise particular aspects of causation and culpability. Also, concentration on culpability is perhaps naturally linked with catharsis since attribution of blame to another may be a natural means of purging the public emotion.

Inquiries do, however, have some advantages in the pursuit of objective explanation. First, as I have already indicated, they can be wide ranging and multi-agency in nature. Proper analysis requires initial *disaggregation* of all the causal roles of various individuals and agencies and inquiries are well placed to pursue this. They can, therefore, pursue limited comprehensive causation ('limited' because they usually do not fully address managerial and service contexts). Secondly, by dint of the 'major event' nature of inquiries *per se*, they can often influence practices and guidelines in an effective 'sudden shift' way which ongoing audit might not achieve. However, this advantage is perhaps limited by the concomitant disadvantage that inquiries seem not fully to take into account macro-contextual factors such as general government policy or the local management of services. Perhaps the routine omission of managers from inquiry panels is strongly indicative of the unwritten terms of reference of all inquiries. Returning to the example of the role of supervision registers, if a clinician places a patient on a register because he fits the criteria of *risk* for such registration, and does so because it is *managerially* required of him, and if the effect on the patient's care is anti-therapeutic (which the psychiatrist might well have known but felt constrained to ignore because the patient satisfied the risk criteria) then it should not be the doctor who is questioned about the apparently clinical (but actually managerial) decision but the manager who imposed supervision registers on the doctor. Indeed, it should ultimately be a member of the Department of Health (perhaps even a minister) who is questioned. Again, there is a potential inherent conflict between the DOH Guidance on Discharge[22] and those parts of the *Mental Health Act 1983* which deal with discharge by Mental Health Review Tribunals. Hence, a clinician is injuncted against discharge to 'unsafe' circumstances by the Guidelines and yet may still feel constrained to discharge the patient because he/she knows that, in law, the patient is not detainable and would, ultimately, likely be discharged by a Tribunal. It would be wholly wrong to criticise a clinician for any failure which resulted from this inherent conflict, which has been constructed by government.

Although inquiries would benefit from introducing managers to their panels, the core inherent weakness of inquiries in the search for truth is not so much in the search itself but in the potential and likely narrow definition of truth. Truth should not, as I have already indicated, be defined in terms of one variable. There must be comprehensive inquiry into the care of a patient. Although inquiries are not necessarily incapable of looking at a number of objectives that were being pursued for a patient by a clinical team, by definition, they are set up to inquire into a single event and therefore into a single variable. However much inquiries may look towards other variables they will tend inherently always to focus excessively on the single event. By contrast, in clinical practice, there ought to be a balancing of the risk of harm to others against other objectives.

In his chapter in this book Carson suggests that an individual mishap should be viewed as the precipitant of a general inquiry into how a particular service was working, rather than as a precipitant of a specific inquiry into the mishap itself. Ask not what did doctor A do on day T but, at the time, how well was *his service* functioning and how well was *the service* (of the whole mental health unit) functioning. Inquiries can make passing reference to service context matters.[23] However, the primary purpose of an inquiry is not to audit a service as a whole and it cannot properly function towards that end.

The failure to learn by Inquiry

Learning is not an event but an ongoing process, and ongoing enquiry is not best pursued by event based inquiries. An inquiry is not only an event but an event which, by dint of a cathartic purpose which requires the 'getting rid' of the whole event (both the homicide and the inquiry), tends to eschew revisiting. That is not to say that it is impossible for individual inquiries to decide to revisit, or cause others to revisit, the scene of their enquiry so as to determine whether specific recommendations have been implemented. However, this is not normal practice. Once the inquiry is over the total catastrophic event is over. Further, there is no mechanism even for documentary accumulation of knowledge from individual ad hoc inquiries, let alone for general service improvement resulting from systematic dissemination of a growing body of inquiry information. Again, the 'event' nature of inquiries estranges it from the process of organisational learning (other than in the 'quantum shift' way which I have already accepted is an advantage of inquiries).

If mandatory inquiries into homicides are to continue then there should be a unified administration of them, even though inquiry members themselves would differ between inquiries. There should also be unified dissemination of a 'composite corporate learning curve', which could be achieved through simple collation and summarising of all inquiry reports. This might even create a 'quasi-audit cycle' in that the most recently updated version of general advice could always be available to services, perhaps even being made mandatorily available(!), so that they could incorporate current knowledge into their own clinical and service audit process.

More radically, I propose that the number of inquiries which have been undertaken, often with similar findings and recommendations, determines that it is unnecessary now to continue to have mandatory inquiries into future homicides. Aside from the fact that there is little *logic* in having mandatory inquiries into homicides while not having such inquiries into suicides by mentally disordered people, the established body of knowledge that is currently available from inquiries determines that future inquiries should be set up only on the basis of 'screening in' those homicides where it is suspected that new learning could be achieved. Refusal to adopt this rational approach would, I suggest, expose the real political purpose of inquiries, laid bare by the demonstration that there was no real purpose in a particular inquiry because it clearly represented, *prima facie*, 'more of the same'. Refusal to abolish mandatory inquiries might also expose a further political objective, that is, to obfuscate the *real* truth of lack of resourcing of community care. A politically embarrassing single event can be turned to effective political *advantage* if the result of the consequent inquiry is to focus on public catharsis and upon the culpability of individual clinicians for what happened. This diverts attention away from inherent structural problems and, indeed, away from the misery of large numbers of mentally ill people who do not harm others and who live in inadequate conditions with inadequate mental health care and who may also be at risk of suicide.

There should now be systematic and comprehensive enquiry into inquiries. This would address what we have learned from them and demonstrate any common themes. By implication, such enquiry might also demonstrate what has, or has not, been achieved through inquiries in terms of improved services. If it were to be demonstrated that later inquiries had identified exactly the same problems present as at some earlier inquiry then this would suggest that there had been little dissemination of inquiry information, or at least little learning from any dissemination that there may have been. If it is not possible to show a service effect for the better arising from inquiries then what is the point in having them?

However, the main argument in favour of abolition of mandatory inquiries is the need to split the four functions of discipline, learning, catharsis and reassurance.[24] This will require public education about the proper comprehensive service audit nature of enquiry into psychiatric homicides. I note that the Ombudsman is *required* to follow up past recommendations in order to ensure that they have been acted upon. Why should there be a lower standard applied to an event which is perceived to be so awful that it is determined currently that society must go beyond ordinary (for example, Ombudsman) procedures and have a cathartic inquiry?

Establishing proper accountability

Theory

A major purpose of inquiries is the reassuring demonstration to the public of proper accountability of public servants for performance of their public duties. However, it is open to serious question whether inquiries are the proper means by which effectively to discipline professionals for professional failure. As I have already indicated, there is a clear distinction between culpability for a breach of professional standards as such and factual causal responsibility for an event which may or may not have arisen through a breach of professional standards. If there is concentration by an inquiry upon the event then this is likely to draw it towards inappropriately implying culpability out of causal responsibility rather than solely looking at potential breaches of professional standards in a proper way. Surely, public accountability of public servants should be to a standard no different from the legal standard which applies to privately employed professionals who are liable either in tort or in contract law. The point is emphasised by the fact that, increasingly, the distinction between private and public employment is becoming blurred, by virtue both of the 'contracting out' of public services and of the use of agencies as a basis for employment, where such agencies are not under direct governmental control. Such blurring is particularly evident now in 'the prison service' (if such an entity indeed still exists) and is becoming increasingly so in aspects of the Health Service, consequent upon the separation of purchasing from provision.

There is a need for an explicitly unified concept of accountability applicable to both private and public servants. This is justified not only on the basis of equity but because of the increasing difficulty in making a clear distinction between public and private employment. Of course, even if culpability were limited by the requirement of demonstrable legal culpability, this might not in itself imply a unified construct. For example, aside from using the *Bolam* test within negligence law to adjudge any possible breach of duty of care, there may be rules within contract or labour law which apply to an employer disciplining an employee, and it is not necessarily the case that these will be directly congruent with the *Bolam* test. Again, professional regulation on the basis of delegated legal authority, for example by the General Medical Council, may not necessarily directly cohere with the *Bolam* test or with concepts in labour law.

I suggest that the proper approach is to leave professional bodies to regulate professional practice. They are ideally suited to judge either/both a person's general professional competence or/and any of his/her particular professional actions against a standard which is defined within, and accepted by, the relevant profession. Use of professional regulatory bodies is inherently just, scientifically logical and also avoids intrusion of extraneous political agenda into what should be a pure purpose. Further, it does not preclude civil action within negligence law, albeit that the results of the two may not be the same.

A further advantage of professional regulation, or indeed of the use of negligence law, is that it emphasises disaggregated individual accountability. The question is simply, 'Did that clinician act within the required standard for that profession in that situation?' The actions and culpabilities of others are irrelevant to the question and should be so. Similarly, the service context is irrelevant to the question other than in modifying the standard which it was *possible* for any clinician to achieve.

Professional regulation is also likely to inhibit the encroachment of extraneous 'managerialism' into professional standards. Specifically in relation to risk management of mentally ill people, it emphasises that this is a clinical construct and not, as might be thought by recent government interventions, a managerial one.

Turning more specifically to negligence law, it is hard to see what is wrong with that tool as a means of ensuring accountability, given that it is based inherently upon recompensing losers for the sins of the truly culpable. It is hard to see what justification there can be for a *de facto* lower standard of culpability, even less a politically contaminated standard. The latter contamination tends to operate in terms of a 'hierarchy of fear'. Ministers transport their political fear down the managerial system ending up with the clinician. There is a need to separate out clinicians, who are individually accountable for their individual actions, from some much more amorphous, aggregated and politically driven notion of managerial accountability, which properly rests upon managers for their overall construction and management of any particular health care service. There should be entirely separate accountability and clinicians should build a clear wall around their own strict professional standards, upon which they will be judged, leaving others to take responsibility for any actions which do not match their managerial standards.

The importance of accountability *to* a professional standard rather than *for* a specific event is emphasised by the clear desirability of disciplining the professional for any breach of the standard even where it did not result in a mishap. Future breaches *could* result in mishaps and so current ones should be addressed. This points not only to the importance of not using inquiries to determine culpability but also towards the advantage of using professional regulatory bodies rather than negligence law, where use of the latter relies upon some damage having resulted from the breach of the duty of care.

Of course, if disaggregation of accountability is not to leave someone or some body unaccountable then there must be *comprehensive* disaggregated accountability. All professionals, managers and even, potentially, Government departments should be seen as potentially accountable. However, *how* the Government can be held to account for policy and finance is much more difficult to conceive of in legal terms. Again, legal bodies such as Mental Health Review Tribunals might properly be seen by some as potentially 'accountable' for their decisions (which may result in harm to the public). However, it is also hard to see how such bodies could be held accountable in this way since they are required to apply a legally determined civil rights approach to detainability rather than a 'case conference' clinical approach, even though that one major piece of research suggests that they are puny defenders of anything other than the formality of civil rights.[25] Perhaps this again emphasises the huge disparity between a proper legal approach and a politically contaminated approach. Tribunals apply the law which should, in theory, make no reference at all to political factors.

Methods

Inquiries are multi-purpose in nature and concurrent pursuit of different purposes is often, perhaps inherently, mutually inconsistent. As Reder and Duncan specifically point out, 'blame limits understanding'. Also, use of inquiries towards a disciplinary function is inherently potentially unjust, largely *because of* the other purposes which an inquiry will concurrently pursue. There may be contamination of the proper standards of accountability and also likely contamination of the proper disaggregation of accountability because, ultimately, the naming of particular professionals as contributory in some way within the aggregate may be inappropriately translated into a presumption that each, or some, are individually responsible according to some nebulous culpability standard.

Injustice may arise where a professional is interviewed by an inquiry ostensibly under the guise of finding out what happened when the procedures are, *de facto,* covertly and effectively disciplinary. Anything which contributes to the professional's confusion about the additional disciplinary role will reduce his/her protection. There may be cosy seductiveness in a private discussion about what happened which may then be reflected ultimately in public humiliation and/or personal resignation.[26] The risk of any criticism within an inquiry report actually being used by others (including the media) towards *de facto* disciplining will be enhanced if there is a very strong need to pursue the purposes of catharsis and/or public reassurance. The need to blame someone may be strong in order to relieve public grief and to reassure the public that they are safe for the future (even though they may not be). This is one of the reasons why our criminal justice system does not allow victims any role in driving Crown prosecution, deciding guilt or deciding punishment. The public in its grief and fear after a homicide is as tainted in its proper judgement as would be an individual victim who was invited to be part of the criminal justice system process against the defendant. Hence, society should not, via inquiries, be vicariously involved in disciplinary proceedings.

However, so long as the use of inquiries continues (towards one or more purposes) they will necessarily have a disciplinary effect. In that case it is imperative that there is maximum protection for professional staff by virtue of the way in which they are set up and by virtue of the rules of procedure which they apply. Hence, anything which avoids cosy seductiveness should be pursued, including avoidance of informal proceedings, avoidance of holding the proceedings in private, confronting the disciplinary issue as a real one in the body of the inquiry, and the keeping of detailed verbatim records of hearings, including records of the reasoning behind the ultimate decisions and recommendations of the inquiry (to allow easy discovery and potential challenge if a professional is disciplined outside the inquiry, such challenge being made on the basis of *proper* standards of culpability, either professionally or legally determined). There should be strict application of the Salmon rule relating to the warning of witnesses. Finally, there should be legal representation of any professional who is in any potential jeopardy from the proceedings of the inquiry. The fact that many will argue, as does Sir Cecil Clothier in this volume, that such comprehensive formality will inhibit the pursuit of truth casts my core argument in sharp relief. If that is the case then clearly inquiries must explicitly pursue *only* the explanation of what happened and avoid any possibility of disciplinary proceedings or effect arising out of their deliberations. Reder and Duncan are right when they call for a separate and sequential approach to disciplinary proceedings and inquiries into what happened.

Specifically as regards process, even if inquiries are bound to be formally inquisitorial they can, and perhaps should, be overtly somewhat adversarial (within the bounds of their formal structure), since that will also provide greatest protection for professionals giving evidence to them. That may be bad for the pursuit of truth (as Clothier argues) but it will be good for justice in relation to professionals.

It might be thought that one way of avoiding findings of 'excess culpability' has been via the inclusion of a psychiatrist on the panel and also by the inclusion of expert psychiatrists in the list of witnesses. However, it is serendipitous which experts might be chosen and, essentially, they are in the position, by analogy, of 'court appointed experts'. It might be more reasonable to extend the representative function on behalf of professional staff to include experts called by them, if such experts can be found who take a view which is of assistance to them. This may sound excessive. However, it again emphasises the injustice of using inquiries inappropriately towards conclusions which are implicitly potentially disciplinary in their impact. There are two types of expertise which may be available either to an inquiry itself or to a vulnerable clinician. First, an expert may comment on general principles of practice. Secondly, he/she may be called as an expert concerning the case itself. Both types of expertise should be available to vulnerable professionals.

In his chapter Clothier argues that private hearings are better than public because people are more likely to tell the truth. However, if public inquiries are attended by increased formality and just protection of professionals then less disadvantage might accrue to them. Further, public inquiries assist the specific function of public catharsis and, more importantly perhaps, the healing of emotional wounds in relatives of the homicide victim. They have the further advantage of linking catharsis with rational debate and the encouragement of social education. Public inquiries may also more rigorously ensure the canvassing of alternative explanations of a mishap, together with alternative views about potential breaches of any duty of care. Most importantly, they also offer a clear forum for the introduction of national or general factors which may be relevant to the mishap in question. It might then even be possible to call government ministers to give evidence about the policy background to any particular service and event within a service. Finally, public enquiries can ensure visibility of proper protection of vulnerable professionals.

Aside from being public, inquiries should also, perhaps, be statutory, particularly having regard to some of the specific legal points offered by Thorold and Trotter in their chapter concerning the requirement of the patient's consent which otherwise applies.

Conclusion

It is time to abolish mandatory inquiries into psychiatric homicides. There was never any substantial justification for treating such events differently from events involving harm to psychiatric patients themselves, other medical accidents or, indeed, deaths arising in ways that are unrelated to mental illness or to medical practice generally. Demonstrably, inquiries are efficient only in pursuing coincidentally one or two purposes and yet they inevitably and inequitably pursue other purposes for which they are wholly unsuited (both in real and equity terms). The pursuit of discipline inhibits the pursuit of explanation *and* discipline is made unjust by the coincidental search for explanation. Explanation and discipline should be uncoupled.

Further, there is no evidence that inquiries do much more than duplicate the findings of their predecessors. Nor is there evidence that there is an accumulated body of knowledge arising out of inquiries which has resulted in improved care.

It would be politically unrealistic to suggest abandoning entirely inquiries into some particular events, including some homicides by mentally ill people. However, there should be clarification of the basis upon which a decision to hold such an inquiry should be taken, perhaps on a background of a *prima facie* hearing. Also, such inquiries should have excluded from their remits any formal influence over the professional careers of those who are being investigated. A natural corollary of this would be, of course, that disciplinary hearings would have to occur prior to any inquiry, whose purpose would then be discovery of what happened, learning from what happened, and public catharsis. It will have to be accepted that public reassurance about accountability might be less easily achieved if there was such uncoupling of discipline from the other purposes, since it would be less visible.

Additionally, there should be a unified administration for all such inquiries which would be responsible not only for administration of further inquiries but also for dissemination of knowledge from previous ones, including dissemination to members of new inquiries.

Above all, crude politics should be removed from the investigation of professional practice. Inquiries should not be available as a means of obfuscating real issues of service design and resourcing, often via the scape-goating of individual clinicians. This is not to say that, sometimes, individual clinicians, agencies, or combinations of agencies have not been at fault, even to the standard of breach of their duty of care, but that is a matter for professional disciplinary bodies and the courts. The finding of some breach of a professional duty of care, at a lower threshold than the law or professional standards set for such breaches, should not be available to be used as a vague smoke screen for avoiding governmental responsibility.

Finally, the strength of my commitment to the views I have expressed in this chapter bears witness to the value of seminars such as the one which gave rise to this publication. Unfocussed unease has, indeed, given way to highly focused and firmly held conviction. There should now be established an ongoing audit of inquiries which, alongside theoretical arguments such as the ones that I have put forward, should be used to determine the future of such inquiries. I believe that the outcome of such an audit is likely to be the conclusion that audit itself is far superior to inquiries in achieving both improved mental health care and increased public safety.

Notes

1. See Department of Health Circular 4 May 1994 (NHS Executive HSG(94)27), with its qualifying criteria; and Appendix A.

2. See the chapter by Reder and Duncan in this book.

3. See the chapter by Carson in this book.

4. *Bolam v Friern Hospital Management Committee* [1957] 1 WLR 582.

5. Häfner H. and Böker W. (1982) *Crimes of Violence by Mentally Abnormal Offenders: The Psychiatric Epidemiological Study in the Federal German Republic*, Cambridge, Cambridge University Press.

6. Monahan J. (1993) 'Mental disorder and violence: another look', in S. Hodgins (ed.) *Mental Disorder and Crime*, London, Sage, at 287-302.

7. Howard M., Conservative Party Conference, 1995.

8. Department of Health (1994) *Introduction of Supervision Registers for Mentally Ill People*, London, HSG (94)5, HMSO.

9. Eastman N.L.G. (1995) 'Anti-therapeutic Community Mental Health Law', *British Medical Journal* 310, 1081-2.

10. Ritchie J., Dick D. and Lingham R. (1994) *The Report of the Inquiry into the Care and Treatment of Christopher Clunis*, North East Thames and South East Thames Regional Health Authorities, HMSO.

11. Such cases typically ultimately settle out-of-court.

12. See *Guardian*, 14 December 1995.

13. See the chapter by Reder and Duncan in this book.

14. See the report of the inquiry into the case of Stephen Laudat which noted the position of a general psychiatrist with a catchment area of 90,000 against the RCP recommendation of 40,000: Woodley L., Dixon K., Lindow V., Oyebode O., Sandford T. and Simblet S. (1995) *The Woodley Team Report: Report of the independent review panel to the East London and the City Health Authority and Newham Council, following a homicide in July 1994 by a person suffering with a severe mental illness*, London, East London and the City Health Authority.

15. See the chapter by Carson in this book.

16. Department of Health (1994) op. cit.

17. It is notable that the Department of Health's 1995 up-date (*Building Bridges*) to the 1994 Executive Guidance now suggests, where appropriate, the appointment of a senior health service manager to an inquiry panel; see also the chapter by Crichton and Sheppard in this book.

18. Bowden P. (1995) 'Critique: Are Inquiries doing more harm than good?', Paper presented at the day seminar *Inquiries after Homicide: Exposition, Expiation or ...*, London, 3 November 1995.

19. Blom-Cooper L., Hally H. and Murphy E. (1995) *The Falling Shadow: One Patient's Mental Health Care 1978-1993*, Duckworth, London.

20. Grounds A. (1995) 'Risk assessment and management in clinical context', in J. Crichton (ed.) *Psychiatric Patient Violence: Risk and Response*, London, Duckworth, at 43-59.

21. See Reder and Duncan in this book.

22. Department of Health (1994) *Guidance on the Discharge of Mentally Disordered People and their Continuing Care in the Community*, HSG(94)27, London, Department of Health.

23. As did the Woodley Report (1995) op. cit.

24. As outlined by Reder and Duncan in their chapter in this book.

25. Peay J. (1989) *Tribunals on Trial: A Study of Decision-Making under the Mental Health Act 1983*, Clarendon Press, Oxford.

26. This point emerged with some force during the discussion of the merits and disadvantages of public vis à vis private hearings at the day seminar *Inquiries after Homicide: Exposition, Expiation or ...*' London, 3 November 1995.

Appendix A

NHS Executive HSG(94)27
and LASSL(94)4

This 'Guidance' was circulated on 10 May 1994 both by the NHS Executive as Health Service Guidelines HSG(94)27 *for action* to Health Service outlets and by the Department of Health as a Local Authority Social Services Letter *for information* to various County, District and Borough Councils and their Social Services Departments as LASSL(94)4.

The circulars draw to the attention of purchasers and providers of NHS care and of local authority social services, guidance on

good practice in the discharge of mentally disordered patients into the community. This is part of the series of initiatives taken under the Secretary of State for Health's 10 point plan, announced in August 1993, to ensure the safe and successful care of mentally ill people who have been in contact with the specialist mental health services. (Para 1 to LASSL(94)4)

Sections from the preamble to the 'Guidance' and paragraphs 33, 34, 35 and 36 are reproduced below.

DEPARTMENT OF HEALTH

GUIDANCE ON THE DISCHARGE OF MENTALLY DISORDERED PEOPLE AND THEIR CONTINUING CARE IN THE COMMUNITY

This guidance seeks to ensure:

- that psychiatric patients are discharged only when and if they are ready to leave hospital;

- that any risk to the public or to patients themselves is minimal and is managed effectively;

- that when patients are discharged they get the support and supervision they need from the responsible agencies.

*

IF THINGS GO WRONG

33. If a violent incident occurs, it is important not only to respond to the immediate needs of the patient and others involved, but in serious cases also to learn lessons for the future. In this event, action by local management must include:

   - an immediate investigation to identify and rectify possible short-comings in operational procedures, with particular reference to the Care Programme Approach. Where court proceedings in relation to the incident have started or are thought likely, legal advice should be sought with a view to ensuring that the investigation does not prejudice those proceedings;

   - if the victim was a child, ie under 18 years of age, the report of the investigation should be forwarded to the Area Child Protection Committee within one month of the incident;

   - incidents involving a death should be reported to the Confidential Inquiry into Homicides and Suicides by Mentally Ill People [telephone and fax nos provided].

34. Additionally, after the completion of any legal proceedings it may be necessary to hold an independent inquiry. **In cases of homicide, it will always be necessary to hold an inquiry which is independent of the providers involved.** The only exception is where the victim is a child and it is considered that the report by the Area Child Protection Committee (see paragraph 33) fully covers the remit of an independent inquiry as set out below.

35. In cases of suicide of mentally ill people in contact with the specialist mental health services, there must be a local multi-disciplinary audit as specified in the *Health of the Nation*.

36. In setting up an independent inquiry the following points should be taken into account:

   i. **the remit of the inquiry** should encompass at least:

      - the care the patient was receiving at the time of the incident;

- the suitability of that care in view of the patient's history and assessed health and social needs;

- the extent to which that care corresponded with statutory obligations, relevant guidance from the Department of Health, and local operational policies;

- the exercise of professional judgement;

- the adequacy of the care plan and its monitoring by the key worker.

ii. **composition of the inquiry panel.** Consideration should be given to appointing a lawyer as chairman. Other members should include a psychiatrist and a senior social services manager and/or a senior nurse. No member of the panel should be employed by bodies responsible for the care of the patient;

iii. **distribution of the inquiry report.** Although it will not always be desirable for the final report to be made public, an undertaking should be given at the start of the inquiry that its main findings will be made available to interested parties.

Note: The Guidance was subject to minor revision in 1995 by the Department of Health in *Building Bridges: A guide to arrangements for inter-agency working for the care and protection of severely mentally ill people.* See paras 5.1.18-21.

Appendix B

Reported, Ongoing and Potential 'Inquiries after Homicide'

These tables have been compiled on the basis of information supplied by the Department of Health, NHS Executive, as of 15 December 1995. The NHS Executive Guidance in respect of 'Inquiries after Homicide' was issued in May 1994, so the first four inquiries below technically pre-date it.

Reported Inquiries

Name	Region	Date of Homicide(s)	Date Report Published
Michael BUCHANAN	N Thames	Sept. 1992	Nov. 1994
Christopher CLUNIS	NE/SE Thames	Dec. 1992	Feb. 1994
David USURO	Trent	Aug. 1993	July 1994
Andrew ROBINSON	South & West	Sept. 1993	Jan. 1995
John Paul ROUS	Oxford/Anglia	Oct. 1993	July 1995*
Alan BOLAND†	N Thames	March 1994	Nov. 1994
Stephen LAUDAT	N Thames	July 1994	Sept. 1995
Kenneth GREY	N Thames	Jan. 1995	Nov. 1995

* Follow up report by Chairman due January 1996
† Committed suicide before trial

'Inquiries after Homicide' – due to report

Name	Region	Date of Homicide(s)	Inquiry Begun
Aidan KENNY	N West	March 1994	Not known, report with DHA
Richard LINFORD	N Thames	Nov. 1994	July 1995
Jason MITCHELL	Anglia/Oxford	Dec. 1994	Sept. 1995*
John RENOUF	S Thames	July 1994	Sept. 1995
Michael FOULKES	S Thames	Dec. 1994	Oct. 1995
Keith TAYLOR	Northern & Yorks	Feb. 1995	Nov. 1995
Shaun ARMSTRONG	Northern & Yorks	1994	Autumn 1995
Frank HAMPSHIRE	N Thames	June 1994	Dec. 1995
Nadish GADHER	N Thames	Sept. 1994	Dec. 1995
Robert VINER†	South & West	April 1995	Report due early 1996
Meurtre KUMBI	N Thames	April 1994	Start date not fixed
Paul MEDLEY	N West	Sept. 1995	Start date not fixed
George HUXLEY	S Thames	June 1995	Start date not fixed

* The Jason Mitchell Inquiry Panel was in a position to be established immediately after pleas of guilty to manslaughter were accepted by the court on 7 July 1995. The Inquiry held its first public session on 2 August 1995 when it announced its terms of reference and proposed procedures. The Inquiry began hearing evidence in September 1995.

† Committed suicide before trial.

Need for 'Inquiry after Homicide' being considered

Name	Region	Date of Homicide(s)
Ms. A.	Anglia/Oxford	Feb. 1994
Mr. B.	S Thames	Nov. 1994

Trial not yet completed

Name	Region	Date of Homicide(s)
Mr. C.	N Thames	Oct. 1994
Mr. D.	S Thames	Dec. 1994
Mr. E.	Northern & Yorks	May 1995
Mr. F.	Northern & Yorks	June 1995
Mr. G.	Northern & Yorks	June 1995
Mr. H.	Northern & Yorks	June 1995
Mr. I.	Anglia/Oxford	Summer 1995
Mr. J.	Northern & Yorks	July 1995
Ms. K.	Northern & Yorks	July 1995
Mr. L.	Trent	Aug. 1995
Ms. M.	South & West	Aug. 1995
Ms. N.	South & West	Sept. 1995
Ms. O.	W Midlands	Sept. 1995
Mr. P.	South & West	Sept. 1995
Mr. Q.	S Thames	Dec. 1995

Index